Beyond the Primary Commodity Trap

Essays on Politics and Poverty in Africa

Uchendu Egbezor

Published by
Adonis & Abbey Publishers Ltd
P.O. Box 43418
London
SE11 4XZ
http://www.adonis-abbey.com
Email: editor@adonis-abbey.com

First Edition,May 2009

British Library Cataloguing-in-Publication Data
A catalogue record for this book is available from the British Library

ISBN: 9781906704261 (PB)/xxxxxxx(HB)

Beyond the Primary Commodity Trap

Essays on Politics and Poverty in Africa

Uchendu Egbezor

Adonis & Abbey
Publishers Ltd

CONTENTS

Beyond the Commodity Trap

Preface and Acknowledgements   **vii**

Introduction   **ix**

Chapter 1
Colonialism and the genesis of the primary commodity trap   **11**

The power struggle   **11**

Knowledge and power: the European problem in Africa   **14**

The colonial Economy: the primary commodity trap and the roots of poverty   **18**

European colonialism and Japanese colonialism   **23**

Colonialism and the African elite   **24**

Chapter 2
Political Independence and the transition to Neo- colonialism   **29**

African Independence and the economy   **32**

The structure of African Economy at independence   **32**

Colonial industrialisation in Africa   **34**

Industrial strategy in Africa   **35**

Political independence and industrialisation   **35**

Neo-colonialism and rural poverty   **39**

Chapter 3
The prevention of Development and the new scramble for Africa   **43**

The impact of IMF policies on Africa   **45**

The new scramble for Africa **48**

African oil and inter – imperialist rivalry **49**

Export credit agencies **50**

NEPAD **54**

Chapter 4
The Arab problem in Africa **57**

Towards Re – Africanisation of North Africa **63**

Chapter 5
Nigeria: an African tragedy **65**

The poverty of leadership in Nigeria **66**

The enduring legacy: power, greed and mediocrity **71**

Chapter 6
Waging war against poverty **74**

The state in Africa **75**

Class struggle and social transformation **79**

Towards a sustained economic Development **82**

Sustainable Development **84**

AID and Development **85**

Chapter 7
The Wages of Failure **89**

The psychological Impact of the humiliation of Africans **91**

The falsification of African consciousness **93**

The future of African people **95**

The road to Renaissance **99**

Revolution in mind set **99**

Revolution in skills **100**

Revolution in values **101**

Index **108**

Preface and Acknowledgements

I have had the opportunity and privilege of meeting and debating with many Africans both from the continent and places such as Latin America and the Caribbean. I have also enjoyed stimulating discussion with Europeans drawn from a range of academic disciplines. Many of these discussions and debates have explored the seeming inability of African nations to consolidate their independence by building viable economies.

A work of this nature, as already indicated, is a collective endeavour. In fact, it will not be possible to name every one who has helped in the preparation of this work. First and foremost, I would like to express my indebtedness to Danielle Oum for her steadfastness, undertaking the initial proof reading and editing my hand written manuscript. Many thanks are also due to Dr Kimani Nehusi and to Clive Fraser (Professor of Economics) who read the initial draft and made extremely helpful comments. I would like to express my appreciation to Kingsley Ogbonda for his support and abiding friendship. I also thank the publisher and editor for their contribution. Above all I would like to thank Dr Daniel Egbezor, Chukwunoye Egbezor and Dickay Egbezor, Mrs Nancy Maduabuchi Egbezor for their unwavering support and encouragement.

The views contained in this work are solely those of the author.

INTRODUCTION

This work analyses the structural sources of the endemic poverty that has reduced Africans to collective failure. Colonialism, neo-colonialism and their legacies are analysed in the context of European and Arab imperialism in Africa. The central thesis of this work is that Africans are faced with the historic challenge of industrialising their economies and developing a new self-reliance. The dream of an African renaissance will remain only a dream until Africans, by their own efforts, face the challenge squarely, and in the process transform themselves.

Chapter 1 provides an analysis of the power struggle between Europeans and Africans , from the trade in enslaved Africans, the colonial occupation of the continent and the consolidation of the colonial division of labour with Africa as supplier of raw materials.

Chapter 2 documents political independence and the transition to neo-colonialism, with particular emphasis on Africa's failure to break the primary commodity trap.

Chapter 3 provides an analysis of the intensification of the power struggle which resulted in the prevention of Africa's development, and the further manifestation of the power struggle in the new scramble for Africa.

Chapter 4 focuses on the Arab expansionist claims on Africa and how this exacerbates / fuels poverty in Africa.

Chapter 5 examines the case study of Nigeria, which despite possessing the human and material resource that could have made it play a pivotal role in the transformation of Africa, symbolises the failure of Africans to control their destiny, the African tragedy.

Chapter 6 explains the need to ensure that the struggle to transform African economies is accompanied by the reclamation of the African mind. Thus the challenge to transform Africa must be inextricably linked to the transformation of the African mentality, from consumers to producers, from imitators to creators.

Chapter 7 looks at Africa's failure to extricate itself from its economic decline and the psychological impact of the power struggle on the African world, both within the continent and throughout the Diaspora. We also point to the road to Africa's renaissance. Whilst acknowledging the differing historical, political and cultural experiences of African peoples, this work primarily focuses on the similarities, particularly in terms of political economy which have contributed to a collective experience that can be justly termed African.

Finally the use of the concept of power struggle is not intended to denote that individual Africans, Arabs and Europeans are enemies, but it must be understood that European and Arabic imperial interests required the imposition of cultural, political and economic practices, generally contrary to the interests of Africans.

CHAPTER 1

COLONIALISM AND THE GENESIS OF THE PRIMARY COMMODITY TRAP

The Power Struggle

For over 1000 years people across Africa's northern borders have not only cast an envious eye on Africa's land and resources, but have done everything in their power to dominate, exploit and expropriate Africans - and what are today generally called Black people – Africans, of their wealth. In the 21st Century BC, Pharaoh Menkare of the Ninth Dynast of Ancient Egypt warned his fellow Africans of the threat across the northern borders. Thus spoke the Pharaoh

> "Lo the Miserable Asiatic
> He is wretched because of the place he's in
> Short of Water, bare of Wood
> Its paths are many and painful because of
> Mountains
> He does not dwell in one place
> Food propels his ego
> He fights since the time of Horus" (1)

A cursory glance at the history of Africa reveals episodes of European attempts at penetration and domination. There was the great clash between the so-called Alexander-The-Great and the Ancient Egyptians. During the great Punic wars there was the epic clash between the Carthaginians and the Romans. More recently, in the relatively modern war between the Moors of Northern Africa and Spain, the Moors suffered defeat in 1492, coinciding with the rise of Spanish colonialism.

By the fourteenth Century, an ascendant Europe increasingly encountered a declining, stagnating Africa. Riding on the crest of its nascent technological and military power, Europe went about imposing its stranglehold on Africa. In 1364 Normans from France were trading and raiding the coast of Cape Verde. The trade and raid to capture and enslave Africans along the coast of Africa escalated to the extent that Italian, Portuguese, Spanish and French traders achieved considerable penetration of the coast of North and West Africa.

In the 1445 the Portuguese began capturing slaves from Goree, off Senegal; by 1447 they had reached the Gambian river and Guinea where the European slave traders encountered one of the first recorded fierce resistance to the slave trade by Africans. (2)

By sixteenth Century Africa, European slave traders and colonialists have ringed Africa with its military forts, such as the Dutch Castle in Cape Town, Elmina in Ghana, Fort Jesus in Mombassa, in Senegal, Guinea and Mali. From these forts and with the connivance of some Africans, Europeans conducted their raids and trades and prepared the ground for direct colonialism, culminating in the Berlin Conference of 1884 which laid the ground rules for the scramble and partitioning of Africa. The partition of Africa was the ultimate expression of European power. J.M MacKenzie in his booklet, *"The Partition of Africa"*, noted that it consolidated a great revolution in the relationship between European and African people, which continues to be felt in Africa to this day. Most African nations will go to war to defend the colonial nations – states within the Berlin-imposed borders. (3) Commenting on the European partition and colonisation of Africa, Chamberlain noted that,

> "clearly Africans were not passive, as was once supposed in the nineteenth century. They were people with a long history who had already held the Europeans at bay for centuries. In the short run, however, the imbalance of technological power was so great that the political decision of the late nineteenth century do seem to have been those of the Europeans". (4)

Europe's ascendancy was in marked contrast to Africa's decline. Thus Africa played a crucial role in Europe's wealth creation, facilitating the development and consolidation of its nascent capitalist system, and to which Asia and the Americas were added from the 16th Century.

In its struggle to impose its political, economic and cultural hegemony on Africa, Europe also deployed some of its best intellectual minds in an assault to weaken Africans' psychologically. Hegel, in his philosophy of History, asserted that the 'Negro' in his African environment,

> "exhibited the natural man in his completely wild and untamed state. There is nothing harmonious with humanity to be found in this type of character". (5) David Humes (1886) concluded that Negroes were "naturally inferior to whites" (6)

Similarly Montesquieu asserted that

> "it is natural to look upon colour as the criterion of human nature....it is impossible for us to suppose these creatures – meaning Africans – to be men...(7).

His opinion of Africans is clearly articulated in his remark that,

> "The greatest part of the people on the coast of Africa are savages and barbarians...they are without industry or arts...they have gold in abundance which they receive immediately from nature. Every civilised state is therefore in a condition to traffic with them to advantage, by raising their esteem for things of no value and receiving a very high price in return."

The Nigerian writer, Chinua Achebe observed that,

> "Europe set up Africa as a foil to Europe, as a place of negation in comparison to Europe's state of Grace" (8)

There developed a body of fantasy and myth about Africa which fossilised into a tradition serving as a storehouse of negative images which until recently remained, at least as an undercurrent, in most European thinking, writing and discussion about Africa. Europe deployed some of its greatest minds against Africa and these scholars propagated the view that African people did not achieve anything, or where there were notable achievements as in Ancient Egypt, it was attributed to outside influence.

Drawing upon the racist tradition of scholarship, racist propagandists and academics engage in intellectual caricature of Black people and fulminate against real and imagined limitations and vices of Black people. No opportunity is spared to lend intellectual credibility to deconstruction of anything that may put Black people in a good light. Constantly reminded of their weaknesses; told they have no intellectual power, that their African God is false, Black people are encouraged to see their existence as void. Such assertions may feel hard to refute against the reality that the Black people are disproportionately surrounded by poverty, that all the modern indices of success predominantly register negatively when weighed against Black people, whether in Africa or in the Diaspora. Racist discourse may be challenged on a theoretical basis but the lack of economic and technological success within Africa and the Diaspora means that, for many, Blackness has become associated with poverty, lack of imagination, low productivity and creativity and ignorance.

But before capitalist colonialism there was no Europe as we know it today. Jaffe (1984) has argued that before capitalist colonialism, Europe was only a collection of feudal, mercantile and tribal towns, farm villages and discrete states and kingdoms vying and warring with each other, just as in Africa, but on a different property basis – private

13

ownership of land. (9) Generally the colonial conquest of Africa in the nineteenth Century, a period which as eloquently expressed by the Emperor Haile Selassie of Ethiopia,

> "...culminated with our continent fettered and bound; with once proud and free people reduced to humiliation and slavery; with Africa's terrain cross-hatched and checker-boarded by artificial and arbitrary boundaries...Africa was market for the produce of other nations and the source of the raw materials with which their factories were fed" (10)

Knowledge and Power : The European Problem in Africa

Europeans, especially people of the more industrialised Western Europe, believe in historical progress and see themselves as its embodiment. The historian, EH Carr, has explained this belief in the following terms,

> "The essence of Man as a rational being is that he develops his potential capacities by accumulating the experience of past generations. Modern man is said to have no larger a brain, and no greater innate capacity of thought, than his ancestors 5000 years ago. But the effectiveness of his thinking has been multiplied many times by learning and incorporating in his experience the experience of the intervening generations...History is progress through the transmission of acquired skills from one generation to another." (11)

Great empires and civilisations, such as Ancient Egypt, Babylon, Persia, Greece, Rome and China have all flourished and suffered decline. These empires made significant contributions to the development and growth of knowledge and skill. But over the last 300 years, Europeans have made very important strides in further development of knowledge and skills, especially in the areas of science and technology. Who would not marvel or be dazzled by the phenomenal inventions such as radio, cars, trains, aeroplanes and helicopters (dubbed by my people of Obukegi, the metal dragonfly)? Who would argue against the mobile phone? Ironically, 80% of the world's known deposit of Coltan, a key mineral in the manufacture of mobile phones, is found in Africa, specifically in the Democratic Republic of Congo. Unfortunately Africans do not have the skill to design and manufacture mobile phones. Armed with knowledge and skills, Europeans not only set out to dominate the rest of the world but also developed a sense of superiority, a belief in the universality of their values and a wilful inability to understand or respect difference.

Arrogating to themselves the power to classify and rename Africans and places in Africa, Europeans developed terms such as negroes, black men, Bushmen, Pygmies; communities became Rhodesia, Gold Coast, Ivory Coast, Nigeria. Similarly slave/Christian names became the order of the day, instead of African names. The European sense of superiority, once allied to technological and economic power, became the basis of the greatest paradox of the last 400 years, the co-existence of European civilisation and criminality on a world-wide scale. The African writer, Chinweizu, explained this quite succinctly, noting that,

"For nearly six centuries now Western Europe and its diaspora have been disturbing the peace of the World. Enlightened through their Renaissance, by the learning of the ancient Mediterranean; armed with the Gun, the making of whose powder they had learned from Chinese firecrackers; equipping their ships with lateen sails, astrolabes and nautical compasses, all invented by the Chinese and transmitted to them by the Arabs; fortified in aggressive spirit by an arrogant, Messianic Christianity of both the popish and protestant varieties; and motivated by the lure of enriching plunder, white hordes have sallied forth from their Western European homelands to explore, assault, loot, occupy, rule and exploit the rest of the World. And even now, the fury of their expansionist assault upon the rest of us has not abated." (12)

By 1846 it is estimated that 52 million Europeans had left their European homelands for other lands. Between1821 and 1932, some 32 million Europeans went to the United States of America, which as is well known, resulted in the ethnic cleansing of the indigenous Americans. Similarly 6.4 million Europeans went to Argentina between 1856 and 1932, 4.4 million to Brazil, 5.2 million to Canada. (13) A visitor, with some humanity, to South and Latin America, could not fail to notice the racist arrogance of the European diaspora who dominate, exploit and treat with contempt the indigenous and non-European peoples of these lands. The defeat of European apartheid in South Africa is still too new to allow for detailed analysis in this work. In his introduction to *Yurugu: An African-Centred Critique of European Cultural Thought and Behaviour*, Professor John Henrik Clarke noted that,

"For the last 500 years the world has been controlled by a form of European nationalism. They have created a concept called the cultural other that has influenced their vision of themselves and other people in their contact with Africans, Asians and people of the Pacific Islands. They have declared most things primitive that they could not understand. The emergence of European or white people as the handlers of world power and their ability to convince millions of people that this is the way things should be is the greatest single propaganda miracle in history." (14)

As Marimba Ani, in her book, *Yurugu: An African-Centred Critique of European Cultural Thought and Behaviour,* has argued,

"the ideology of progress allowed Europeans to speak with impunity of 'uncivilised' and 'superior' races in the nineteenth century and later allowed them to speak of 'developed', 'advanced' and 'modern' nations. Generally, Europeans have very little resources of their own. But, in their view, they have the 'expertise' and the 'drive' that allows them to make 'proper use' of the resources of others. Thus colonialism and neo-colonialism in Africa, South African Apartheid, European settlers' expropriation of the best land in Zimbabwe are all justified in the European mind. Thus the ideology of progress justifies and vindicates European attitude towards Africa's resources and political integrity." (15)

An intrinsic element in the European idea of progress is the practice of 'rhetorical ethics', that is the ability to say the opposite of what is really meant, to pretend to be what one is not, to profess values that do not motivate one's behaviour towards others. Rhetorical ethics is essentially the profession and proclamation of values that are not indicative of actual behaviour towards others; it is the elevation of hypocrisy into a political art and weapon of deceit.

Marimba writes that,

"The European rhetorical ethic is precisely that, purely rhetorical, and, as such, has its own origins as a creation for export; i.e., for the political intercultural activity of the European. It is designed to create an image that will prevent others from successfully anticipating European behaviour and its objective is to encourage non-strategic (i.e., naïve, rather than successful) political behaviour on the part of others. (This is the same as 'non-political' behaviour) It is designed to sell, to dupe, to promote European nationalistic objectives." (16)

Again, as Marimba Ani explains,

"The rhetorical ethic is made possible by the fact that hypocrisy as a mode of behaviour is a valued theme in European life; the same hypocritical behaviour that its presence sanctions...European culture is constructed in such a way that successful survival within it discourages honesty and directness and encourages dishonesty and deceit – the ability to appear to be something other than what one is; to hide one's 'self', one's motives and intent. People who are duped by others and related to a projected image are considered

16

fools...Hypocrisy in this way becomes not a negative personality trait, not immoral or abnormal behaviour, but it is both expected and cultivated. It is considered to be a crucial ingredient of 'sophistication', a European good." (17)

One needs look no further than the European controllers of world power, through agencies such as the United Nations' Security Council, the International Monetary Fund, World Bank, and North Atlantic Treaty Organisation to see the full machination of their power. For the Europeans concepts such as Democracy and human right mean what their nationalist agenda demands. In other words, these concepts are often used as a mask to cover up European self-interests, applied to put pressure on a perceived opponent. The ideology of progress, allied to European mastery of technology, enables Europeans to control concept and images of people and places. There is a school of thought, which believes that colonialism was good for Africa. Proponents of this view argue that Africa had no modern development, no literacy, except those provided by Arabic/Islamic hegemony and that it took colonisation for the development of modern education, hospitals and amenities etc. As we have already noted elsewhere in this work, some of Europe's best minds waged a relentless intellectual war on Africans, a war which continues but is now waged with less crudity. Hegel, for example stated that Africa is not a historical part of the world,

> "it has no movements or development to exhibit. Historical movements in it – that is in its northern part – belong to the Asiatic or European world. Carthage displayed there an important transitionary phase of civilisation; but, as a Phoenician colony, it belongs to Asia. Egypt will be considered in reference to its Western phase, but it does not belong to the African spirit. What we properly understand by Africa is the unhistorical, undeveloped spirit, still involved in the conditions of mere nature nature, and which had to be presented here only as on the threshold of world history" (18)

Thus Africans accept images of Africa seen from the eyes of Europe's Henry Norton and David Livingstone, salvation is through a white Christ, the great white father paternalism and the lazy African who did nothing before slavery and created nothing historically. Thus Africans accept their branding and categorisation into the so-called Black Africa, Sub-Saharan Africa, Bushmen, Bantus – terminologies which many educated Africans accept and reproduce unthinkingly and uncritically (19). But it is on the political economy of Africa that the power struggle has had the most devastating and enduring legacy.

The Colonial Economy: The Primary Commodity Trap and The Roots of Poverty

Whilst Africa's pre-colonial economy was pre-dominated by peasant Agriculture, there were highly developed techniques of working, for example, bronze, tanned and dyed leathers. Generally there were sophisticated forms of exchange based on gold which were mined in Africa. There were well developed trade networks linking North and West Africa. There are historians who, in comparing the developed areas of Africa with Europe of the same period, note that the difference between the two lay not in the level of technological development but in the scale produced. (20)

Before the industrial revolution, most European trade was in primary products such as silk, cotton, sugar and spices, although Europe could export some small arms which were hardly better than those made in the East, such as China. (21) Europe undermined much of Africa's local industry; for example, local African textile business was destroyed by bringing Indian textiles to Africa. Europe destroyed African commerce and mining industry, already disrupted by the slave wars and trade.

Whilst Europeans became more aggressive, more expansionist and more dynamic in producing new forms of goods, Africans failed to meet the manufacturing challenge, neither innovating new products nor increasing the scale at which their existing industries manufactured goods.

European technology in the fifteenth century was not totally superior to that obtained in Africa and other parts of the world, but it did have certain features which were not only advantageous to Europe but decisive in the encounter between Europe and Africa: Shipping and Guns. As Rodney has shown, in the early centuries of trade the economic penetration of Africa was to continue to the extent that by the time the Europeans imposed colonial rule Africa was concentrating almost entirely on the export of raw materials, unlike Europe which exported manufactures. While Europe invented and innovated, Africa stagnated. Rodney wrote,

> The fifteenth century saw the multiplication of the primary accumulation of European Capitalism: and Africa played the most important part of the process as the principal arena of European Colonialism, the very genesis and foundation of the capitalist system. From the turn of the sixteenth Century the Americas and Asia were added to the foundation, and out of this totality arose capitalism and modern Europe itself. (22)

While the people of Obukegi still have their lands and the social formation remains communalistic, the European system became based on private property, European peasants driven off their lands and the land violently expropriated by the feudal lords. Within Europe, the subjugation of the Irish and the Welsh by the English was a forerunner to the colonisation of Africa. Africa had its share of internal strife and the tragedy of the slave trade. But as Teresa Hayter noted,

> "the accumulation of wealth in Europe and North America and their industrial and technological advance, are relatively recent phenomena."(23)

It was in the 19th Century that the expansion in the other European, North American and later Japanese wealth and productive capacity took place. As Eric Hobsbawn has observed with regards to the industrial revolution which was to change the face of Europe,

> "For the first time in human history, the shackles were taken off the productive power of human societies, which henceforth became capable of the constant, rapid and up to the present, limitless multiplication of men, goods and services...No previous society had been able to break through the ceiling which a pre-industrial society structure, defective science and technology, and consequently periodic breakdown, famine and death imposed upon production." (24)

In this period, Europe did not enjoy a higher standard of living than Africa and it is worth remembering that the concept of "Third or Developing World" is relatively new. However, while Europe pressed its foot hard on the accelerator, Africa went into reverse. The colonial education system, designed to create a cadre of African clerks to service the colonial system, African by birth but European in outlook, laid the foundation for the neo-colonial order and the corrupt leaderships that characterised post-colonial, "independent" African states. Obukegi and the rest of Africa were to be absorbed into a world capitalist system. This new system brought about the creation of the latter day nation states of Africa. But in order to integrate Africa into Europe's global capitalist system the colonial powers imposed wide-scale use of European currency as a means of exchange, displacing many of the local currency systems already in place, such as cowries and manila. The colonial powers imposed taxes which were paid in European currency. The compulsory requirement for taxes to be paid in European currency was a very significant and, indeed a critical measure. It not only led to European money becoming the predominant means of exchange and

19

measure of value, but also forced many people to leave their villages to seek wage labour. The power of the colonial state which was organised like a military dictatorship, the imposition of European currency allied with Western European technical progress spelled the doom of African entrepreneurs. It enabled the Europeans to ruin many of their African competitors. As Ake noted:

> "...the monetary system not only helped to create a capitalist economy, but also a capitalist economy structurally dependent on foreign economics. Thus the colonial currency was tied to that of the colonising power, and money supply was determined mainly by the social and economic forces in the metropole, particularly the demand for the colony's exports. The dependence of the colony's prosperity on the export demand of the metropole re-inforced not only the export orientation of the colony, so that it became complementary to the metropole economy, but it also compelled its specialisation on primary products" (25)

This specialisation in primary products has not changed despite the fact that African countries have been independent for more than three decades.

The disarticulation of the African economy is another feature of the colonial legacy that is critical to understanding the roots of the endemic poverty in Africa.

In essence, an economy is disarticulated when its different sectors do not complement each other. For example the agricultural sector may not be supported by the manufacturing sector and so agriculture's basic technological needs are met through the importing of tractors, incubators and feeds etc. An example of this structural problem is demonstrated by Nigeria's huge petroleum oil industry, an intensive high technology-dependent enclave economy in which not only is all the technology imported but also the key engineers and scientists running the industry are non-Africans.

Although the colonial state built some roads, water resources, railways, electrical power and established administration structures; these were mainly to facilitate the extraction of primary resource from Africa. Whatever investment that was made in the colonies was very basic; a minimum input for maximum output. This approach was perfectly rational since from the colonialist perspective, the African colonies now existed as a supplier of raw materials. Wealth was extracted from African produce and spent in the Western countries. Moreover while African exports were primary products with little or no local processing, refining or manufacture, most consumer goods in Africa, especially in colonial areas such as Lagos, Port Harcourt,

Abidjan, Accra were imported from the European countries. The African colonial cities became islands of growth in contrast to the villages, which were oceans of stagnation. The dichotomy between the African urban life and village/ rural life remains as we write. There is a case for arguing that the colonial state deliberately discouraged the development of industry in the colonies to oblige the African colonies to depend exclusively on the Western European capitalist countries for manufactured products, and to remain a market for the goods manufactured in the Western countries.

To live in the colonial city was to be regarded as modern while to live in the village was to be backward, for modern read Europe and for backward read Africa. In fact this dichotomy was to provoke the ire of the Kenyan novelist Ngugi wa Thiong'o. In an essay titled *"The crisis of culture in Africa today"* he notes that

> "the crisis of culture in Africa has too often been seen in terms of a conflict between tradition and modernity; the rural and the urban; and the clash of values consequently engendered by that dichotomy. In this schema, the urban (industry, technology, electronic etc), is identified with modernity; the rural (subsistence agriculture, economic backwardness, etc) with tradition" (26)

By 1900 Africa's place in the Western constructed capitalist system had become consolidated as a supplier of raw materials to feed Europe's rapidly growing industry. Thus Africa's position as a supplier of raw materials but an importer of Western industrial goods became entrenched and remains so at the time of writing. Worst of all, African countries depended generally on one or two major export crops which commonly account for over 50% of all exports and support 50% of all imports as the table below shows.

Country	Crop/Commodity	Percentage of export earning		
		1977	1979	2006
Burundi	Coffee, Tea, Gold	94	93	
Mauritius	Sugar	94	63	
Gambia	Groundnuts, Fish	90		
Uganda	Coffee, Fish	82	27	
Chad	Cotton, Gum, Livestock	80		
Ethiopia	Coffee, Leather	75	69	
Rwanda	Coffee, Tea	73	71	
Eq. Guinea	Cocoa, Oil, Wood	66		
Somalia	Live Animals	61	71	
G. Bissou	Cashew nuts, Fish	60		
Sudan	Cotton, Oil, Sesame Seeds	60	65	
Ghana	Cocoa	61		
Kenya	Coffee	54	27	
Swaziland	Sugar	54		
Lesotho	Wool	50		
Mali	Cotton, Diamonds, Gold, Livestock	50	47	
Senegal	Groundnuts	50	37	
Nigeria	Crude Oil	80	80	

Source B.Dinham and C.Hines (1983) p187

While opening Africa up as a market for the Western capitalist manufactured goods, colonialism imposed on Africa an economic structure in which the African colonies depended on one or two products for trade with the Western nations. Thus the African countries were heavily affected by the vagaries of the economic policies of the Western capitalist countries. While Africa was incorporated into the Western capitalist system, there were hardly any indigenous owners of capital and the development of capitalism in Africa had been foreclosed by European conquest. The colonialists did not attempt to design industries in line with the tastes and practices of the local population, rather the colonialists directed their efforts at changing the local consumption habits to conform to those which the new industries catered for, those of the colonialist countries. As already noted the European interest in Africa lay primarily in Africa as a source of raw material and as a market for selling Western European manufacture. Alongside the European colonial rulers and European merchants, there were some local merchants and other middlemen, some times African but more usually of Asian or Lebanese/Levantine origin, who were the local agents of foreign companies. Michael Barratt Brown noted that, "the colonies existed for the colonial trade; and it was in the very nature of the colonial trade that not only was wealth drawn from Africa to be spent in Europe and not in Africa, but also that most even of the consumer goods in the African cities had to be imported from Europe. Exports were of primary products with little or no processing refining or manufacture." (27)

Generally the proportion of the final value of African Products that remained in the continent was about 25%. The more the market prices of these primary products fell the less the final value of what remained. The problems associated with the instability of the price of Africa's primary products continued unabated; it is the primary source of poverty in Africa.

For a majority of Africa's peasants such as the Ogba people, who are one of the clans that inhabit the Eastern part of Nigeria, the incorporation into the European created and controlled capitalist system made the community dependent upon one cash crop – palm produce - for the income to buy foreign goods. While a considerable quantity of the palm produce was consumed locally as cooking oil and for the manufacture of soap and skin lotion, the surplus was sold to buying agents of the foreign monopolies such as the Royal Niger Company. The money that was made from the sale of palm produce was to pay various taxes (paid in colonial currency), and to buy the Western pharmaceutical products and medicines which were beginning to replace the traditional African ones. So began the process whereby most of Africa consumed what they do not produce and produced what they do not consume.

European colonialism and Japanese colonialism

European colonial policies in Africa were in contrast to Japan's colonial policies in South East Asian countries such as South Korea and Taiwan. Whilst not suggesting that the Japanese were altruistic or benevolent towards their colonial territories, it can be argued that there were clear long term economic benefits to having been colonised by Japan.

Japan was a late starter on the path of industrialisation and colonialism and was greatly influenced by the Rheinish model of political economy. This required serious state intervention in the development and guidance of the national economy (28) and is particularly evident in Japanese economic policy on its colonies such as South Korea and Taiwan. Japan handed down to its colonies some of the necessary technologies and overseas markets for them to manufacture and export goods at a level of technology which Japan had moved out of. Moreover, Government departments within South Korea and Taiwan have worked together with their Japanese counterparts as mentors to step up the technology of their industrial companies, stage by stage with Japan's technical and financial support. (29)

In effect, whilst the colonial state in South Korea and Taiwan, for example, were developmental in orientation, African colonial states were essentially extractive. As we shall see in the next chapter, the impact of this extractive colonialism continues today. To appreciate the scale of this impact let us briefly look at the colonial education of the African elite.

Colonialism and the African Elite

Slavery and colonialism generally shattered the self confidence of Africans, especially the elites. It foisted on Africa an elite class that is intellectually and psychologically dependent on Europe; that is alienated from the African masses, for all their protests to the contrary. Cheikh Hamidou Kane in his novel, *"Ambiguous Adventure"* captured its essence when he wrote

"A hundred years ago "our grandfather, along with all the inhabitants of this countryside, was awakened on morning by an uproar arising from the river. He took his gun and, followed by all the elite of the region he flung himself upon the newcomers...our grandfather, and the elite of the country with him, was defeated. Why? How? Only the newcomers know. We must ask them. We must go to learn from them the art of conquering without being in the right. Furthermore, the conflict has not yet ceased. The foreign school is the new form of the war which those who have come here are waging."

Chancellor Williams, in his book, *"The Destruction of Black Civilisation,"* put it even more succinctly as he noted that no matter what the factual data were, all the books written about Blacks by their conquerors reflected the conquerors' viewpoints and considering how thorough going was the capture of the minds of Black people, it is not surprising that many black scholars, politicians and the Black elite generally, still faithfully follow in the footsteps of their European masters. (30).

Africa's budding elite who went to the colonial schools received training organised by the colonial state or the missionary and were generally indoctrinated with the colonial historiography. At the time of the struggle for Independence, most of the movements were led by European- educated elites - Dr Danquah, Dr Kwame Nkrumah and Dr

Koffi Busia (Ghana), Dr Nnamdi Azikiwe and Chief Obafemi Awolowo. (Nigeria). It was even worse in the French colonised African countries. Ahmadou Ahiddjo (Cameroun), Leopold Senghor (Senegal) and Houphouet Boigny (Ivory Coast) were such colonial products.

Dr Nwachukwuike Iwe, a Nigerian academic, typifies the Europeanised thinking too often displayed by Western educated African academics in his book, *"Christianity, Culture and Colonialism in Africa"*. In the chapter titled "The Impact of Western Civilisation on Our Culture" Iwe waxes lyrical on the superiority of western culture,

> "The Western world is in possession of civilisation absolutely secular…Here is a civilisation characterised by intellectual maturity, politico-institutional stability, advanced science and technology, greater appreciation of human dignity, values and fundamental freedoms and progressive socio-economic equilibrium and advancement." (31)

Turning his pen on Africa, Dr Iwe is less complimentary,

> "spiritually, our culture is intensely religious and ethically orientated to the point of superstition or fanaticism at times….socially, our culture is characterised by self-reliant, collective egoism, mass illiteracy and lack of modern social institutions and amenities….Economically, the characteristic features of our culture are – primitive agricultural ways and methods of life, super-abundance of raw materials, incipient industrialisation." (32)

Another such example is that of Mr Areoye Oyebola who in 1976 published a very controversial book. Oyebola contended that

> "Throughout history, the black man has shown an appalling loss and lack of integrity in position and intellect and the thinking world cannot fail to be struck by the negativity, opportunism and parochialism of black people's activities." (33)

Further more he argues that

> "As black people, we have no country to be proud of in terms of its great inventions and discoveries, its technical equipment and political power…No Black Country has solved the problem of poverty among a great majority of its citizens. None has found any concrete solutions to the problem of poor nutrition, endemic diseases, inadequate basic education and infrastructural facilities." (34)

The sources of Areoye Oyebola's comment lies, arguably, in his acceptance of Western historiography, re-enforced by the endemic political and economic failures of most post-colonial Africa. It is also a case of an inability to contextualise Africa's socio-economic problems, as evidenced by his negative hand- wringing approach.

Even the army officers whose mutinous activities were to cause so much death and destruction in Africa were trained by the West: majors C.K. Nzeoqwu, Theophilus Danjuma, Murtala Mohammed (Nigeria), Colonel Akwasi Afrifa, Lt Col H.K. Acheampong (Ghana), Sergeant Gnassingbe Eyadema (Togo), Mobutu Sese Seko (Zaire),Bokassa and Idi Amin were all trained outside of Africa. Colonel Afrifa, who was one of the key players in the overthrow of the pan Africanist Kwame Nkrumah of Ghana, revealed in his autobiography the extent to which these budding elite were affected by their colonial education,

"Sandhurst gave us independent thinking, tolerance and a liberal outlook. I entered Sandhurst as a boy and left as a soldier. No one cared whether one was a prince, lord, commoner, foreigner, Muslim or Blackman...I left Sandhurst, crossed the wish stream, looked back at my old school and was filled with boundless gratitude...Now I look back on Sandhurst with nostalgia." (35)

Similarly in his preface to Afrifa's autobiography, Dr Busia, who became Ghana's prime minister after Nkrumah's overthrow, describes Afrifa as

"..a citizen with an impassioned faith in the value of democracy, and in the British Commonwealth. He has the courage, rare in these days of Flaming African nationalism, to express his gratitude for the training he received at Sandhurst, and his admiration for the democratic institution of Britain." (36)

The African sociologist Dr J.A. Sofola(1978) has argued that many educated Nigerians exhibit a feeling of cultural inferiority in many ways, for example, whenever African past is mentioned...they are immediately prone to refer to those things that would appear primitive and derogatory and never see the good and equally positive ones...To many such Nigerians anything of value is made in Europe:- to enjoy the prestige associated with being perceived as well-educated then one's degree must be from London; household appliances should be imported from overseas even if similar items were made locally or in Nigerian factories. In fact, for most Nigerian elite, the terms "modern" or "progressive" are synonymous with "European" or "Western". Such views can reach farcical extremes, such as proposals for African cities to be re-planned as the new London or Paris or adopting the architectural designs, which are more suitable to the temperate climate.(37) "Colonial mentality", a phrase popularised in Nigeria by national musician Fela Kuti, pervades Africa.

Kwame Appiah (1996) explained that whilst European students have largely internalised a system of value that prohibits them from seeing the culture of Africa as a source of value to them, African students raised without relativism expect Westerners to value there own cultural products because they are, by some objective standards superior. Appiah argues that these sociological facts which reflect asymmetries of cultural power, have profound consequences. (38)

In the final analysis the story of African politics and economics, from sixteenth century onwards has been one of subordination and dependence. In the developing of an African elite colonialism engendered a mentality of dependency and parasitism that continues today. It is a historical truism that the worst defeat that could be inflicted upon a people is the defeat of the mind. The greatest struggle facing African people on the continent and within the broader diaspora is the reclamation of the African mind. To understand this is to understand African problems today.

References

(1)Jacob Carruthers, 23; 1999
(2)Hosea Jaffe, 43; 1984
(3)J.M. MacKenzie, 2; 1984
(4)M.E.Chambers, 98; 1974)
(5)Hegel, 93; 1956 Philosophy of History,*(Cited in Carruthers 1999)*
(6)David Humes, 1886 *(Cited in Carruthers 1999)*
(7)Montesquieu, 238-332; 1881*(Cited in Carruthers 1999)*
(8)Chinua Achebe, *Hopes and Impedements*, 2; 1982
(9) Hosea Jaffe, Opcit , 45; 1984
(10)Excerpts from the speech of the late Haile Selassie of Ethiopia to the Summit Conference of African Leaders, May 25, 1963
(11) E.H. Carr, 114; 1964
(12)Chinweizu, 3;1974
(13)Encylopedia Brittanica, 1968 *(Cited in Galbraith 1999)*
J.H. Clarke, *Introduction to Yurugu* 1992
(14) Marimba, Ani, 508; 1994
(15) Ani, Opcit 316; 1994
(17) Ani, Opcit 316; 1994
(18) Carruthers, Opcit 23, 1999
(19)Ben-Jochannan, *preface to First Edition*, 41; 1980
(20)Walter Rodney, 42; 1983

(21)See Woytinskiy – *World Commerce and Government;* 1955

(22) Rodney, Opcitt, 42; 1983

(23)Teresa Hayter, 47; 1981

(24)Eric Hobsbawn, *28;* 1964

(25) Claude Ake, *35;* 1981

(26)Ngugi Wathiong, speech delivered to Oxford University African Society; 1982

(27)Michael Baratt Brown, *51;* 1996

(28) For an introductory discussion of the Rheinish Model of political economy, see Barat Brown, Models of Political Economy; 1984

(29) See Chapter 5 of Jon Holiday and Govan McCormack; 1973

(30) See   Chancellor Williams, The Destruction of Black Civilisation; 1987,

(31) Iwe, Christianity, Culture and Colonialism in Africa, *68;* undated

(32)Iwe, Opcit, *10;* 1975

(33)Oyebola, *13;* 1975

(34) Oyebola, Opcit, *10;* 1975

(35) Afrifa, the Ghana Coup, *50-52,* cited in the Chinweizu; 1974

(36) Koffi Busia, preface to the Ghana coup

(37)Sofola, *41,* 1978

(38)Kwame Appiah, In My Father's House, 1996

CHAPTER TWO

POLITICAL INDEPENDENCE AND THE TRANSITION TO NEO-COLONIALISM

At the end of the Second World War, Africa was largely the preserve of four European powers, Portugal, France, Britain and Belgium. Until 1945, there was no serious challenge to their rule but all this was to change from the end of the Second World War. The 1960s was remarkable for the intensification of African people's nationalist struggle, including the decolonisation wars that swept from Algeria, Kenya, Guinea Bissau, Angola, Mozambique, Zimbabwe and ultimately the triumph of African nationalism over the forces of European nationalism and racism in South Africa. In 1961 the All African People's Conference, held in Cairo, recognised that neo-colonialism posed a serious threat to the newly independent nations of Africa. In fact, the conference foresaw that the newly independent countries were quickly becoming the victims of an indirect and subtle form of control and domination. Dr Nkrumah, in his work, "Neo-colonialism, the Last Stage of Imperialism ", warned of Africa's imminent transition to neo-colonialism, a system he foresaw as more sinister and dangerous than colonialism. Nkrumah observed that,

> "faced with the militant peoples of the ex-colonial territories…imperialism simply switches tactics. Without a qualm, it dispenses with its flags, and even certain of its more hated expatriate officials. This means, so it claims, that it is 'giving' independence to its former subjects to be followed by 'aid' for their development. Under cover of such phrases, however, it devised innumerable ways to accomplish objectives formerly achieved by naked colonialism. It is the sum total of these modern attempts to perpetuate colonialism while at the same time talking about 'freedom' which has become known as 'neo-colonialism' "(1)

It was then becoming increasingly clear that the colonial countries of Britain, France, Portugal and Belgium were not just going to let the African countries consolidate their independence. In addition, on the horizon lurked an even greater formidable threat to African independence than the fading colonial powers, the US.

A growing number of Western political analysts, and African scholars influenced by them, are uneasy with the term 'neo-colonialism' They query its relevance, given that most African States have been independent for more than three decades, preferring terminologies such as pre-bendalism, clientelism, and neo-patrimonialism to describe

African politics. For example, Nicholas Van de Walle, one of the leading American Africanist scholars, has argued that of the different terminologies used to characterise political systems in which clientelism is endemic, the most commonly accepted and useful is neo-patrimonialism. He notes that a neo-patrimonialist state has a constitutional order, including written law which clearly demarcates public and private functions, but that the constitutional order is constantly thwarted and undermined by officeholders appropriating public resource for private use. (2) Neo-patrimonialism describes the prevalence of corruption and nepotism in Africa. However, whilst these terminologies have generated some insight into the characteristics of African politics, they do not explain the source, nor do they offer a solution. For most Western analysts, such terminologies place the problem of poverty in Africa squarely on the shoulders of the African, ignoring or playing down the interaction between the demands of Western political and economic needs and the opportunism of Africa's political elite. The new terminologies rightly blame Africans for the failure of their political system but, at the same time, absolve Western countries of blame for their constant meddling in African politics and economic affairs. Nkrumah's analysis of neo-colonialism in Africa remains relevant today in understanding African politics, as discussed in more detail in Chapter 3.

From 1958 to 1962 not only were there calls for African unity but numerous attempts were made to achieve it. Ideologically two broad currents of Pan-Africanism were discernable. African leaders such as Kwame Nkrumah and Sekou Toure advocated revolutionary Pan-Africanism, insisting upon immediate unification of Africa along broadly socialist lines. Revolutionary Pan-Africanism's strength during these years was its just and popular cause, the independence and unification of Africa. Revolutionary Pan-Africanism enjoyed the backing of progressive forces throughout the world and the support of the African masses. It could be argued that one of Nkrumah's enduring contributions to the struggle of Africans for emancipation is his theoretical work.

Opposed to Revolutionary Pan-Africanism were those whom Elenga Mbuyinga labelled Demagogic Pan-Africanists. (3) This brand of Pan-Africanism aimed at maintaining the status-quo created by colonialism. Its main strength at that time was the support it received from colonial powers and their agents, such as Houphouet Boigny (Ivory Coast). The African governments that militantly advocated the unification and independence of Africa were overthrown one after another. Kwame Nkrumah's government was overthrown by military coup in February 1966. Pan-Africanist leaders such as Ahmed Ben Bella

(Algeria), and Patrice Lumumba (Congo Kinshasa) were all overthrown. Recent de-classified documents from some of the colonial countries have revealed the extent of Western interference in African affairs. Those Pan-African leaders, such as Sekou Toure (Guinea), Julius Nyerere (Tanzania) who survived, did so under conditions of incessant political and economic pressure from the colonial countries of France, Belgium, Portugal and the US.

In his foreword to Reginald H. Green and Ann Seidman's book, *Unity or Poverty, the Economics of Pan-Africanism*, Thomas Hodgkin noted that

> ".whether ruling parties have survived or whether they have been replaced by military regimes, the trend has been towards a consolida-tion of the power of those forces and interests which are essentially ter-ritorialist, conservative and pro-Western in their attitude." (4)

Commenting on the rising tide of counterrevolution in Africa, Kwame Nkrumah noted in his book, *"Dark Days in Ghana"*, that

> "An all-out war is being waged against the progressive independent states.
> Where the more subtle methods of economic pressure and political subversion have failed to achieve the desired results, there has been resort to violence in order to promote a change of regime and prepare the way for the establishment of a puppet Government. Fragmented into so many separate states, many of them weak and economically non-viable, coup d'etat have been relatively easy to arrange in Africa. All that has been needed was a small force of disciplined men to seize the key points of the Capital City and to arrest the existing political leadership. In the planning and implementing of these coups, there have always been just sufficient numbers of dissatisfied and ambitious army officers and politicians willing to co-operate in making the whole operation possible" (5)

However, the blame for Africa's current economic situation cannot be attributed solely to imperialism. Africa's march towards liberation, independence and unity was subverted by the collusion between external and internal profiteers. When European colonialists established colonial states they replaced the autonomous basis of inter-ethnic relations with the power of the State, throwing together different ethnic groups with little regard to their social structures and cultural sensibilities, aggressive manipulation of political power promoting the financial interests of the elite within dominant ethnic groups. The political rivalry and inter-ethnic clashes that resulted from this process facilitated the intervention of the colonial power; the colonialists were always ready to support whatever factions would protect their own interests.

African Independence and the Economy

The 1960s were remarkable for the intensification of the African people's nationalist struggle, including the Liberation Wars that would ultimately lead to the liberation of Angola, Mozambique, Namibia, Zimbabwe and most recently South Africa. But political independence is inadequate when it is accompanied by inherited and continued economic dependence for markets, goods, capital, technical skills and personnel on the same imperialist states and their firms. National sovereignty is an illusion in the global world order without the scientific, technological and manufacturing foundations. A state must have an economy that is geared towards production for national needs and this requires productive and technical capability. It must be able to generate nationally the bulk of investment and skilled manpower which are necessary for rapid and sustained growth, failing which it will remain dependant on other more economically powerful states and their powerful economic interests. Despite incessant proclamations about "the struggle for economic independence", almost all the post-colonial regimes have proved totally incapable of making much progress in the direction of providing for the most elementary needs of their populations. As Africa's submission to the Special Session of the United Nations' General Assembly in 1986 summed it up,

> "....vicious inter-reaction between excruciating poverty and abysmally low level of productivity in an environment characterised by serious deficiencies in basic and social infrastructure most especially the physical capital, research capabilities, technological know-how and human resource development that are indispensable to an integrated and dynamic economy." (6)

The Structure of African Economies at Independence

African economies, at Independence were clearly dependent. The condition of the African economies was neatly articulated by Green and Seidman. They noted that:

> 1) "A high ratio of exports to national products with exports limited to a few goods virtually all of which are the products of unskilled labour, climate and/or mineral resources;
>
> 2) A high ratio of imports to national products, with the bulk of man-ufactured consumer goods and virtually all capital goods imported;

3) Capital imports, including re-invested foreign profits at a high level in relation to total domestic investment

4) Foreign trade concentrated and conducted with a few economically much larger states

5) Foreign investment and aid sources equally concentrated, and most or all foreign investment directed to building export capacity rather than national market-orientated development

6) Small national markets, which render a radical shift in production patterns to reduce dependence difficult and costly

7) Inadequate public sector revenues and low domestic private savings, which hamper the financing of even those changes in the structure of production consistent with small sized national markets

8) Limited technical and managerial capacity, necessitating the importation of a substantial number of teachers, managers and technicians as well as virtually all new technology and applied research." (7)

More than 30 years since the above study was published, Africa remains heavily dependent on primary commodities as a source of export earnings, with severe consequences for national economic development and the people's welfare. Since the 1960s many developing countries have registered significant structural changes; many are now moving into manufacture. Some studies have suggested that about 70 percent of exports from developing countries are in manufacture. At around 30 per cent in 2000, the share of manufactured exports in the continent's total merchandise exports had increased by only 10 percentage point. The continent's share in world merchandise exports fell from 6.3 per cent in 1980 to 2.5 per cent in 2000 in value terms. Similarly, its share of total developing country merchandise exports fell to almost 8 per cent in 2000 while the share of world manufactured exports remained a little below 1 per cent. (8) As the last sentence in the above quotation reveals, after more than 30 years of Independence Africa's share of world manufactured exports remained no more than 1 per cent. Now, if we discount the economy of South Africa, which was developed and controlled by European settlers, the figure is pathetic by any stretch of the imagination.

The dismal performance of Africa contrasts sharply with the much celebrated South East Asian countries whose share of global merchandise exports increased from 18 per cent in 1980 to 22 per cent in 2000 while its share of global manufactured trade reached 21.5 per cent in 2000 (9)

Colonial Industrialisation in Africa

Industrialisation, however achieved, is without doubt, one of the fundamental conditions for Africa's escape from underdevelopment; it is the root cause of Africa's domination and humiliation by foreign powers. Industrialisation presumes the acquisition of technological capability which underpins the creations and developments of industry. Few would argue that today, technology is the glue that binds production, distribution and markets. Technology connects producers, designers and consumers, and enables mainly Western capital and cultural commodities to move around the globe in a remorseless quest for profit. Therefore, the rapid development of technology and the creation of industries by any means is an absolute imperative to reduce underdevelopment. Africa's industrial process and technological development pre-dated colonialism.

The attitude of colonialists to the industrialisation of Africa was clearly articulated by Jules Miline, a French minister, who, according to Rene Dumont, in March 8 1899, argued that the colonialists dislodged in advance any signs of industrial development in the colonies to oblige the colonies to look exclusively to the imperialist countries for manufactured products and to fulfil, by force if necessary, their natural function, that of a market reserved by right to the mother countries' industry. (10) Along the same lines, the British Governor of Egypt from 1883 to 1907 declared,

> "the policy of the Government may be summed up thus: (1) export of cotton to Europe...; (2) import of textile products manufactured abroad: nothing else enters the Government's intentions, nor will it protect the Egyptian from the cotton industry." (11)

The imperialist countries benefit greatly from African countries' concentration on the production of primary products. As we shall also see, most Western investments that flow into Africa are concentrated on the extraction of raw materials: crude petroleum, iron and cobalt. Dr Henry Kissinger in 1976 at the fourth UNCTAD in Nairobi, argued that,

> "a special effort must be made to expand the production and exports of primary products of developing countries.." (12)

Contrary to what Europeans (the West) may profess publicly, there is a case for arguing that they have a vested interest in keeping Africa as a producer of primary products, not withstanding Independence. In fact most of Western policy, as we shall see in due course, is aimed at keeping Africa as underdeveloped primary producers and a market for Western manufacture. In this scheme of things, African leaders have colluded in this perverse and global division of labour which perpetually condemns Africans to tilling land and hewing stone.

Industrial Strategy in Africa

Early colonial attempts to build modern industries in Africa can be traced to 1930-40 through what some economists have labelled "import substitution industrialisation". (13) Bade Onimode has suggested that the prolonged export depression of 1929-45, and the stimulation of the colonial economies in the war period, as part of the world capitalist reconstruction, gave the initial stimulus for the introduction of import-substitution industrialisation. (ii)

The colonist built some industries, which were mainly primary products and raw material processing plants and infrastructures for transporting raw materials from the hinterland to the coast. The colonialist applied the import substitution strategy (ISI) in Africa. One of the main characteristics of ISI is its heavy concentration on the manufacture of consumer goods to the total neglect of capital goods. It concentrated on the production of such simple consumer goods as beer, soft drinks and textiles. The colonialist completely excluded the manufacture of capital goods, such as electrical goods, machinery and tools. Most of the ISI industries were owned by Western multinational companies and were characterised by (1) their dependence on technologies imported from the colonial countries; (2) high capital intensity: over-reliance on technology rather than the abundant African labour;(3) low manufacturing value-added (14). As would be expected, it was not in the interest of the Western multinationals or the economic planners of the colonialist countries to use African input, except raw material and unskilled labour, or pass their technical skill to Africans in any meaningful or systematic way. Most of the technology used for ISI was imported from the industrialised imperialist countries. Therefore, they were not suitable for Africa, with its abundance of labour. In other words its relative capital intensive operations led to underutilisation of labour, resulting in unemployment. What is more, the manufacturing value added in Africa remains very low. The fundamental question is what would Africa's post-colonial elite do to transform their economy?

Political Independence and Industrialisation

Whilst the emerging post-colonial elite recognised that there was a massive technological gap between Europe and Africa; that manufacturing industry and construction were the key to combating Africa's scientific and technological backwardness. But Africa's leaders failed to lead by personal example, through self-discipline and integrity; they displayed a lack of will and foresight to pursue the mixture of programmes that would have placed the continent on the path of technological and industrial development. Most of the initial planning of the industrial sector was undertaken by the colonial foreign experts. Therefore they influenced greatly the pattern of attempts of industrialisation of the newly Independent nation states in Africa. Project planning and execution was carried out with deliberately little or no participation by Africans. The African political elite, who suffered from inferiority complex and colonial mentality, rarely consulted their own people, nor bothered to engage Africans in any meaningful dialogue. Worst of all many African engineers, technicians and artisans were totally excluded and marginalised, without opportunity to modernise and improve their skills. Thus, in the fields of science, technology and engineering, Africans remain the least skilled. Consciously or unconsciously, the African political elite collude in denying Africans adequate opportunity to develop the necessary engineering and manufacturing skills. African nations have not only failed to develop technology, including the skill to develop and create things, but have failed to develop the scientific base (tradition) that supplies technology. There are many faculties of science and technology, and universities of technology but these are only paper tigers and window dressing because there is no organic link between these academies and the technological needs of society. Most of these academies exist to give the impression that African Governments are taking development seriously. The first, and arguably only, serious effort by an African nation to develop indigenous technological and industrial skill was during the Nigerian Civil War (1967-1970). The break-away republic of Biafra, blocked by the Federal army of Nigeria was forced to become self-reliant by the exigencies of the war. It took the exigency of war to force Ibos (Biafra) to form the Research and Product Unit (RAP) which led the effort to develop and manufacture equipment. Dr Pius Okigbo, one of Nigeria's leading economists noted that the Biafran Directorate of Research and Productivity (RAP) which was working under extremely difficult conditions, produced effectively useable military equipment and supplies, such as tanks, rockets, mortars, anti-aircraft guns, landmines and anti-tank weapons from materials obtained purely from local source. The Research and Productivity Unit also fabricated agricultural implements, durable consumer goods, including spare parts and equipment, communication and telephone systems. The Biafran engineers built the Uli airport, which provided the lifeline between Biafra and the outside world. It ensured the steady flow of water and electricity to towns and rural areas that became temporarily the base of military operations throughout the war. (15) Colonel Joseph Achuzia, one of Biafra'a very successful field commanders and an electrical engineer by profession, wrote in his memoirs, *"Requiem Biafra"*,

> "Biafra as a scientific centre, that saw the most concerted input in scientific research by Africans, can no longer be neglected."(16)

The real reason for Africa's tragic state of underdevelopment is that Africans are being politically and economically held down by Western imperialism and a neo-colonial African political elite. Nothing demonstrates the delusion and the bankruptcy of neo-colonialism than the historically urban-based investment programme which imposes super-express highways, multi-storey buildings, luxury goods assembly industries in countries without basic feeder roads, clinics, cheap drinking water, simple shelter and factories to produce the national population's basic needs. In fact as far back as 1962, the French agronomist drew attention to the perverse neo-colonial development programme of African nations. He observed that,

> "China has received a great deal less aid from the Soviet Union than Africa from Europe, and it has been in credits, not outright grants. Emphasis was placed on factory equipment and raw materials, not school and highway construction. Tropical Africa can never catch up to China in this century if it continues to hold itself aloof from the economic imperatives of development." (17)

Because of Africa's failure to develop or create indigenous technology and technological skill, most modern industries are like foreign bodies in African society, relying mainly on foreign experts and imported spare parts. Nothing is more pathetic, and indeed clearly shows the bankruptcy of Africa's neo-colonial political economy than the spate of derelict industrial plants. African Governments borrow money to buy expensive foreign industrial plants only to abandon such plants because of lack of spare parts and the cost of maintenance. In 1973, Zaire, under the leadership of the late ultra corrupt General Mobutu, bought modern cotton–treating plants in US for 7.5 million dollars. None of the plants ever worked because the planners omitted the high-tech electronic control system. It was money gone down the drain. Again the Zaire regime bought a TV communication complex for the Voice of Zaire, at 110 million dollars in 1980. The president of the manufacturing company was Phillipe Giscard d'Estaing, the first cousin of the then president of France, Valerie Giscard D'Estaing. The system broke down immediately and rarely worked. Nigeria, as we shall see, is the tragedy of Africa, and has spent over 2.8 billion pounds opening a steel factory in Ajaokuta but the factory has produced nothing. In 1980 Tanzania borrowed 22 million pounds to build a shoe factory with foreign expertise, only to find out that it lacked suitable leather for the factory. The industrial plant closed down in 1990 – a waste of resources.

Africa's level of technical expertise is far lower than any other continent among the developing nations. The low level of technical expertise affects productivity and productive activities that are fundamental to raising living standards. Although rich in many essential resources, Africa does not have the technical skill to turn these resources into finished consumer products to sell in domestic and international markets. A prime example being that despite Coltan, a raw material essential to the manufacture of mobile phones, being located in Africa, the mass up-take of mobile phones by Africans has not been matched by involvement in the technology to manufacture mobile phones.

As happened in colonial times, Africa's raw materials are exported outside the continent where they are turned into finished consumer products to be re-sold to Africans. Thus African economies depend on the export of a few primary products whose prices are very volatile. A primary reason for the volatility is that the western trans-national corporations exert enormous control over commodity markets and price setting. From 1980-2000 prices of cotton fell 47 per cent, cocoa by 71 per cent, coffee by 64 per cent and sugar by 77 per cent. Between 1986 and 1989 Sub-Saharan Africa lost about 56 billion US dollars, 15-16 per cent of the GDP. Despite the dismal, debilitating, economic conditions, African people's desire and dependence on Western, and now Asian, manufacture, is greater than ever: cars, electricity, electronic gadgets, mobile phones, computers. Africans are slaves of Western technology. In my village, Obukegi, only one family owned a car in the 1960s, most people travelled by bicycle. By the 1970s three families in Obukegi owned cars; by 1979 there were 6 cars and 4 motorcycles in the village. But between 1990 and 2004 there were more than twenty cars in the village owned by youths. Today, anyone who does not drive a Mercedes or a Four-Wheel drive then is regarded as a nobody. Thus the competition for consumption of Western goods has become the essence of the economy but with very little thought to how to create, organise and manage industry that would provide these goods domestically. In order to fuel the sickening consumption of Western, and now Asian, manufacture, Africa's elite are most inventive and imaginative when organising schemes and scams that facilitate the stealing and transfer of capital from Africa to Western banks. Thus following to the letter the biblical injunction that to him who has, more shall be given, the UK newspaper, *The Observer* on 29 September 2002 reported the case of Citibank of America's link to the corrupt president Omar Bongo, who presides over the rentier* state of Gabon in West Africa. Similarly, the City Bank of America was censured because of its collaboration with the family of General Sani Abacha, Nigeria's former dictator, who stole over 1.3 billion dollars from Nigeria. According to the report, no fewer than 23 UK banks facilitated the transfer of money by General Abacha's family into the West. Unlike other parts of the world such as Japan, China and South East Asian countries, where the political elite worked to generate a great deal of domestic saving for investment within their countries, for the transformation of their economies and the development of their industries, Africa's political elite and retainers rob the people of Africa to feed their own greed. Large sums of money are stolen by those whose oath of office was to safeguard and manage Africa's resources wisely. Collier, Hoffler and Pattillow have shown that about 40 per cent of the stock of Africa's savings is held outside Africa (18). Despite the scarcity of capital, Africa's elite, Western banks, and their Asian and Lebanese associates, rob and transfer annually about 15 billion US dollars; the euphemism for it is "capital flight". The American magazine, *National Enquirer*, in February 1993, revealed that 3,000 Nigerian officials have stashed away 33 billion US dollars in Swiss banks. The late General Mobutu of Congo stole more than 5 billion dollars from the Congo, enough money to pay his country's foreign debt.

The gross mismanagement of the African economy by the undeclared alliance between the African elite and their foreign advisors led to massive borrowing and the catastrophic debt burden upon Africans.

Neo-colonialism and Rural Poverty

At the time of political independence in the 1960s, 85 per cent of Africa's population lived in the villages, rural ancestral lands, and 70 per cent still live in the villages. The traditional village/peasant economy was generally self-sufficient because the basic pre-requisites of existence, such as food, clothing and shelter, came from the land. Villages such as Obukegi and clans such as Ogba were generally self-sufficient in basic necessities. But the traditional peasant economy suffers from what the American economist John Kenneth Galbraith called "equilibrium of poverty". Galbraith has observed that, "since life is near the bare level of subsistence, there is no saving. Without saving and the resulting capital investment, there can be, from within the agricultural economy itself, no investment in improved agricultural technology, in irrigation, hybrid seeds, pesticides, fertilisers, improved machine cultivation. Without such investment there can be no improvement in income that allows of saving and further investment." (19)

Thus traditional peasant economy, though stable, was stagnant; people have lived that way and have invariably come to terms with this existence. People lived in villages where there was no electricity, radio or modern technological gadgets. It could be argued that the traditional villages were characterised by equilibrium of poverty.

Colonialism disturbed and undermined the equilibrium of the traditional peasant economy. As we have already noted, not only did the colonialist force the villagers to produce cash crops for export to the colonial countries, but introduced into the colonial cities commodities such as radios, bicycles etc, which then filtered into the villages. Suddenly the budding Elite who made money from their connection with the colonial rulers returned to the villages with consumer goods which they exhibited with pride. Out of the traditional peasant areas emerged the African petit bourgeoisie who, as middle-men, were dependent and parasitic upon the European connection. The colonialists and the Africa's budding elite, who were generally articulate in the "new colonial knowledge" manipulated and betrayed the African poor, especially rural women, by not transforming the rural economy.

The political elite aided by the western countries continue to squeeze out resources from the African masses, especially the peasants, to support their opulent lifestyles. Meanwhile consumerism has placed a stranglehold on the people of Africa, at all levels of society. Everybody, even in the remotest African hamlet, aspires and craves to own cars, videos, houses built with imported modern gadgets and seek treatment in Western type hospitals and take Western medicines produced by Western pharmacists in preference to visiting the village doctor or herbalist. Now, where is the money to pay for all these if these African countries continue to rely on a few primary products which they sell unprocessed to the industrialised countries? . According to the UN, nearly half of Sub-Saharan Africa, 600 million people, lives on less than 1 dollar a day. Life expectancy is declining, improvements in healthcare and education have been minimal in the last decade. One third of all Sub-Saharan African children are now malnourished. In this time of the knowledge-based economy, 40 per cent of the children have no access to

40

primary education and school enrolment rates are falling. There is now, not just a growing intensification of rural poverty, but a new more debilitating type of poverty which threatens to turn the African Village into a wasteland of deforestation. There is an increasing population which is imposing dangerous pressure on the environment. Grazing lands and peasant farmland which have historically supplied the villages their needs are diminishing both in productivity and quantity available for farming. This is resulting in a growing destitution of the peasantry. Whereas in the pre-colonial and colonial period, there was enough land to provide the peasants with subsistence means of livelihood, there is now a growing population who have no access to land or the land available is of small quantity and low in quality to provide the peasantry with subsistence but sustainable livelihood. The population pressure on the land, with the antiquated farming techniques, is such that there are increasing mass of youths who are unable to earn a living from the traditional way of the ancestors. Worst of all there are no industries or factories to absorb these youths. Without industry, without resources of energy except unskilled manpower, without improved methods of cultivation, Africa faced a vicious circle. There is a case for arguing that the debilitating rural poverty, especially food insecurity, is fuelling rampant inter-community wars in Africa as the control of resources become a matter of life and death struggle. The African peasants are rarely given vocational training; even those who managed to acquire vocational skills through self-effort or through family support find that all their efforts frustrated by lack of factories and industries to absorb them. Many migrate to the urban areas where poverty and penury equally await them; the most desperate risking all by embarking on a reckless exodus to the West.

Meanwhile, the global corporate interests, which are dominated by the West, allied to African politicians and the elite, continue to squeeze, every ounce of resources from the African peasantry and working class to pay for imports and service debts. For the majority of the villagers, abject poverty has become their fate.

References

(1)Nkrumah, Neocolonialism: The Last Stage of Imperialism, 239; 1965
(2)Nicolas van de Walle, 51; 2001
(3)M'buyinga, Pan Africanism or Neo-Colonialism, 42; 1975
(4)Thomas Hodgkins, Foreword to Unity or Poverty; 1968
(5)Nkrumah, 49; Dark Days in Ghana, 1968
(6)ECA/OUA, Addis Ababa, 4; 1986

(7)Green and Seidman, Unity or Poverty, *94;* 1968

(8) UNCTAD: Economic Development in Africa: Trade Performance and Commodity Dependence, *3-4;* 2003

(9)UNCTAD: IBID

(10)Rene Dumont, False Start in Africa, *51;* 1981

(11)Teresa Hayter, The Creation of World Poverty, *49;* 1981

(12)UNCTAD: Economic Development, *67;* 2003

(13)Stewart, Lall and Wangwe, *241;* 1992

(14)Onimode, *128;* 1988

(15)Pius Okigbo, Ahiajoku Lecture, 1986

(16)Joe Achuzia, *I;* 1986

(17)Dumont, Opcit, *47;* 1981

(18)Collier, Hoffler and Pattilow, 2001

(19)Galbraith, *49,* 1983

Chapter 3

THE PREVENTION OF DEVELOPMENT AND THE NEW SCRAMBLE FOR AFRICA

In his foreword to the book, *Our Continent, Our Future* (Mkandawire and Soludo, 1999) KY Amoaka, noted that a major irony of African development history is that the theories and models employed have largely come from outside the continent. He argues that no other region of the world has been so dominated by external ideas and models. (1)

If any international organisation clearly exposed Africa's failure to control and shape its destiny, and clearly demonstrate the determination of Western Imperialism to maintain its stranglehold on Africa, that organisation is the International Monetary Fund (IMF).The organising of the post Second World War international system was largely through the medium of the International agencies: the United Nations, International Monetary Fund, World Bank and others. The IMF and its sister organisation, World Bank were established in 1944 during the Bretton Wood Conference. The aim of the IMF was to finance short-term balance of payment adjustments for member nations. It was hoped that such a measure would, among other things, avoid exchange rate instability and competitive monetary policies, as happened before the Second World War. The number of votes on IMF's executive board depends on the size of the financial contribution of the individual member countries. Decision making powers lie ultimately with the Western industrialised nations, especially the United States of America.

It is significant that the IMF was set up to help rebuild and stabilise the Western industrialised countries devastated by war. The founding members of the organisation and the early recipients of its help were highly skilled and industrialised, structurally balanced economies and well-tuned to free market competition, in contrast to the African countries. The Western nations' economies needed steady sources of finance and market to counter the aftermath of the War. Hayter and Watson (1985) (2) noted that one of the key roles of the IMF is to control and scrutinise overall drawing and to have discretion to promote what it considered to be appropriate domestic policies in its member countries. They noted that the organisation, clearly reflecting the interest of the United States of America as the dominant power, began to see the Fund's major objective as the promotion of Free Trade and

Free Access to the markets of Europe and the Third World.

Stiglitz (2002), the former Chief Economist at the World Bank and former Chairman of USA President's Council of economic advisors, stated that whilst the ideas and intention behind the creation of the international economic institution were good ones, over the years it has evolved to become something very different. Stiglitz argued that the Keynesian orientation of the IMF, which recognised that markets do fail and also recognised a role for Government in job creation, was replaced by the free market orthodoxy of the 1980s, part of a new Washington consensus. The consensus is between the IMF, World Bank and the US treasury about the appropriate policies for developing countries. Stiglitz has noted that,

> "the underlying problem of the IMF and other international economic institutions is the problem of Governance. Who decides what they do. The institutions are dominated not just by the wealthiest industrial countries, but also by commercial and financial interests in those countries; and the policies of the institutions naturally reflect this. While almost all the activities of the IMF and the World Bank today are in the developing world, they are led by representatives from the industrialised nations. The institutions are not representative of the nations they serve." (3)

The IMF does not encourage democratic debate or popular discussion of its policies. Meetings and negotiations are usually held behind closed doors. They are generally held secretly between a few top officials of the ministry of Finance of the adjusting country and officials of the World Bank/IMF. Thus policies which fundamentally affect the future of African peoples are implemented with little input from them, and sometimes against the popular opposition of African people. The elitist and bureaucratic implementation of these programmes means there is no mass mobilisation and popular participation of abroad section of the population. The African economist, Onimode (1992) (4) stated that repressive dissent management has been employed as a mechanism for the denial of accountability in the adjusting countries. He notes that the mechanisms of repression include military intervention to break adjustment stalemate and brutal killings by the police and military during IMF riots. The use of state brutality to counter popular protest against IMF policies tends to reinforce state violence and abuse of human rights.

Yusuf Bangura (1986) (5) argued that the overthrow of the democratic Government in Nigeria in 1983 by the Nigerian Army and the violent repression, especially against students and trade unions, was in order to break the impasse between the civilian Government and the IMF. For the finance ministers and treasury secretaries of the imperialist countries and their financial oligarchies the last thing they want is a lively democratic debate about alternative economic strategies to development. This strategy suits the African elite for whom mass poverty in Africa may not be a failure but is a pre-requisite for their accumulation of wealth, their privileges and their social, political and economic domination.

It is worthy of note that between1981 and1982 the US and Britain (the chief proponents of the Anglo-Saxon world order) and other Western countries raised their interests, forcing up the cost of borrowing for third world countries and consequently, precipitating the world debt crisis. The US, Britain and other western countries embarked on deflationary economic policies which largely caused the collapse of world commodity prices that severely affected Africa. The debt crisis provided the European countries (the West) with the opportunity to address the threat of prospective new industrial Third World countries by forcing them to restructure their economies and pressurising them to accept greater integration into the global economy, thereby advancing Western economic interests and making easier the penetration of Western multinationals.

The impact of IMF Policies on Africa

One of the requirements of the Structural Adjustment Programme (SAP) is that African states cut back on social spending so that money is saved to pay back foreign debts as well as qualify for further loans. Invariably this leads to austerity measures, which in turn leads to a reduction in social expenditure such as education, medical care and rural development projects. Stein and Nafziger (1991) (7) have recorded that Tanzania, for example, introduced school fees for primary schools in 1986, exacerbating a trend, which resulted in a serious decline in school attendance. In 1984 school enrolment was 84 per cent, in 1986 it was 69 per cent but by 1987 school enrolment for 6-11 year olds had fallen to 66 per cent. Under the Structural Adjustment Programme (SAP) the Government of Senegal cut education expenditure even though 67 per cent of Senegalese adults were illiterate (Yassine Fall 1998). Under the auspices of SAP, the Kenyan Government abolished free primary education and introduced school fees of 44 shillings per month which is beyond the reach of many poor Kenyans.

Healthcare expenses have been cut in many African countries. Under IMF pressure, Zambia increased registration fees at health centres. This led to a decline in immunisation programmes and to an increase in diseases such as Whooping Cough and Polio. In Senegal healthcare expenditure was reduced under Structural Adjustment Programmes: In 1990 the Government spent 2.3 per cent of the GDP on healthcare instead of the 9 per cent recommended by the World Health Organisation (WHO).

Structural Adjustment was often accompanied by inflation and unemployment and, consequently, acute poverty. Not only does the reduction in workers' purchasing power affect the families of the wage earners since it reduces the ability of families to buy basic necessities, it also affects the economy generally. It leads to a serious drop in the capacity for utilisation of available goods and services because of a fall in demand. Stern and Nafziger (1991) have argued that low wages exacerbated illness, absenteeism, poor morale, a decline in physical dexterity and a reduction in workers' commitment to invest in labour skills. In the case of Tanzania, it has been noted that between 1981 and 1986, when the Government came to terms with the IMF, wage levels fell by 50 per cent, and then by a further 33 per cent from 1986 to the end of 1988. Even agriculture, such a fundamental part of the African economy, has not been spared the SAP scourge. Tanzania, in order to qualify as a worthy client of IMF, cut subsidies on agriculture, increasing the price of agricultural inputs. Ross Hammond (1998) has argued that Tanzania faced severe food shortages due in part to the removal of subsidies on fertilisers. Contrast this policy with the fact that the Western nations subsidise their agriculture. Between 1986 and 1988 the European Union gave agricultural subsidies in the region of 110 billion dollars. The US subsidised its own agriculture in the region of 69 billion US dollars (8).

Another way the SAP hurt Africa and exacerbated Africa's condition of mass poverty is its impact on the industries. The Structural Adjustment Programmes have also had the effect of destroying or undermining the existing but patchy African industries. Currency devaluation and the tightening of credit have had adverse consequences for the industrial sector. The cost of obtaining foreign and domestic funds increases with devaluation. It also resulted in a large proportion of unused supplier credits because of the burden of paying back such loans, which in the context of devaluations makes repayment very oppressive. Funduga (1989) has noted that the condition created by the structural adjustment programmes encouraged companies to shift from production to trading activities. He argues that the enforced liberalisation in most cases usually destroys small-scale industries, causing unemployment and acute conditions of poverty.

The structural adjustment programmes have generally compounded Africa's debt problem. Ghana, which implemented the SAP, took on debts which grew from 1.1 billion dollars in 1984 to 2.4

billion dollars in 1986. The debt service ratio grew from 9 per cent in 1981 to about 61 per cent in 1987. Africa now owes Western creditors in the region of 250 billion dollars. Every African person owed Western creditors in the region of £377. (9) Africa spends in the region of 60 per cent of its GNP to service debts, even before paying principal. This was what provoked Ngugi Wa Thiongo, Kenyan author and political activist into declaring that,

> "from the days of slavery and colonisation to the present, Africa has always acted as a ragged trousered philanthropist to the Western world. It is absolutely criminal that Africa should spend over 60 per cent of its GNP to service debts, even before paying the principal. Africa thus becomes a net exporter of much needed capital alongside its exports of raw materials."

But Africans are robbed of their wealth not just by the Western banks, but by African elites, who hide their money in Western banks. The United Nations Economic Commission for Africa in its report, "African Alternative Framework", noted that "there is mounting evidence that stabilisation and structural adjustment programmes are rending the fabric of the African society. Worst still, their severest impact is on the vulnerable groups in society – children, women and the aged – who constitute two-thirds of the population. (7) But worst of all, as Fantu Cheru (1992) has argued, the ideologically obsessed adjustment policies, while improving output for export crops, aggravate poverty, income inequalities and environmental degradation. The structural adjustment programmes contribute to deforestation and soil erosion by directing resources, money and valuable personnel toward the export producing sector for short-term gains. This problem is particularly acute among countries that border the Sahara Desert such as Niger, Mali, Chad, Ethiopia, and Bukina Faso. Commenting on the presence of IMF in Africa, Oswaldo De Rivero (2001) made the depressing observation that

> "In Africa the result of adjustment policies has been more deleterious and even less certain. Africa is the developing region in which the World Bank's structural adjustment programmes have been most generally applied. Since 1982, when the debt crisis began, in Africa alone, 162 programmes have been implemented compared with just 126 in all the rest of the developing world. Some African countries applied as many as four adjustment programmes between 1983 and 1993. In contrast to Latin America, Africa has not attracted even short-term speculative foreign capital. On the contrary, its status as exporter of practically nothing but raw materials and basic commodities has been reinforced under the structural adjustment programmes...

Adjustment has then enmeshed Africa even more tightly in the basic products trap...Africa has entered the new Millennium as a continent full of dysfunctional national economies out of sync with the Global economy." (11)

One of the main arguments, often advanced by Africa's orthodox free market protagonists and IMF sponsors is that Africa needs foreign investment; it is argued that it brings skills, know-how and international marketing channels, which would boost the process of development and enable Africa to catch up. But between 1983 and 2002, 59 per cent of the total FDI that flowed into Sub- Saharan Africa, i.e. excluding Egypt, Algeria, Morocco, Tunisia and Libya went to three countries: Angola (13 per cent), Nigeria (23 per cent) and South Africa (23 per cent). These investments went mainly to the extraction of raw materials such as petroleum oil and diamonds. This pattern of foreign investment only reinforces Africa's dependence on basic/primary commodities from which the continent is unlikely to extricate itself unless drastic political and economic measures are taken so that there is massive investment across a wide range of productive industries throughout the whole economy.

The New Scramble for Africa

Despite more than four decades of political independence the reality remains that Africa's trade relationship with the rest of the world is dominated by basic commodities and the extraction of basic or primary commodities. As already hinted elsewhere in this work, Africa possessed in large quantities all of the thirteen basic industrial raw materials needed by modern economies. Cobalt is absolutely essential for building jet airplanes. The United States produces no Cobalt but Zaire and Zambia do. The United States is 88 per cent dependent on imported Bauxite, 95 per cent dependent on imported Manganese, 90 percent dependent on imported Nickel and 100 per cent dependent on imported Tin. The West relies also on Africa's strategic materials such as Aluminium, Zinc, Chromium, Iron, Lead, Tungsten and Coltan, vital for the production of mobile phones and laptop computers. (12) All these basic materials are exported raw because Africa has neither the technical ability nor the industries to process and turn these materials into consumer goods.

Since the 1990s Petroleum Oil and Gas accounted for more than 50 per cent of Africa's exports and 65 per cent of all foreign direct investment. (13) The Petroleum Oil industry is a capital and technology intensive industry, dominated by giant multinational companies whose budget and global political clout dwarfs the African countries in which they operate. African Governments are only a small part of the forces and web of interests that shape the dynamics of oil production and marketing in Africa. In fact, the main power brokers are international financial institutions, such as the World Bank and the International Monetary Fund (IMF), as well as the Western Governments such as the US, UK and France, the home countries of the multinational companies. A powerful convergence of interests between African governments, international oil companies, international institutions and the Western governments is propelling the rush to exploit Africa's oil reserves. Sub-Saharan Africa is home to eight oil exporters – Nigeria, Angola, Congo Brazzaville, Gabon, Equatorial Guinea, Cameroun, Chad, the Democratic Republic of Congo and Sudan. Several other exporters are entering the field and both large and small companies are snapping up exploration licences from Mauritania to Madagascar. Governments across the continent, including Sierra Leone, Senegal, Niger and Uganda, are hoping that they too can cash in on the oil bonanza. It is apparent that at this rate Africa will become one huge oil drilling camp.

It is estimated that Africa's oil production will jump from 3.8 million BPD to 6.8 million BDP in 2008. West Africa's growth potential is considered to be greater than that of Russia, the Caspian or South America. While African Governments ultimately make the decisions regarding the exploitation of petroleum in their territory, as we have noted, they operate in an international environment, conditioned by very powerful actors. African oil has been traditionally dominated by Elf (French), Shell (Anglo-Dutch) and to a lesser extent, Chevron Texaco (US based). For years the scramble for African oil has been taking on a more American character. New fields are being aggressively pursued by Exxon Mobil, Chevron Texaco and, to a lesser extent, by independents such as American Hess, Vanco, Ocean and Marathon. Chevron Texaco in 2002 stated that it had invested 5 billion dollars in the past five years in African oil and would spend 20 billion dollars more in the next five years. Exxon Mobil proposes to spend 15 billion dollars in Angola in the next four years and 25 billion dollars across Africa during the next decade. Non-Western companies such as Malaysia's state-owned company, Petronas, and the Chinese National Petroleum Company are also increasing their presence in the continent, most notably in Chad and Sudan. (14)

African Oil and Inter-Imperialist Rivalry

From the early 1960s, even with political Independence, inter-imperialist rivalry and competition for Africa's primary commodities have not diminished. Oil has been no exception. African leaders, at the national and regional levels, have often taken advantage of the inter-imperialist rivalry. G. Nder (1992) has suggested, for example, that the overthrow and death of Chad's former president Ngarta Tombalbaye in April 1975 was linked to economic rivalry

> "oil and the war of influence France and the USA were engaged in, were somehow related to some of Chad's upsets. Tombalbayes's anti-French diatribes alone do not explain his downfall and asassination. Many witnesses to his reign are convinced he signed his own death warrant the day he offered exploration permits to an American firm. (15)

In May 1995, the United States of America's late Commerce Secretary, Ron Brown, during a visit in Senegal which is the heart of so-called Francophone Africa, declared,

> "The United States will no longer concede African markets to traditional colonial powers."(16)

The United States former Secretary of State, Christopher Warren, in his 1996 visit to Senegal, harangued France for treating Africa as its "private domain". (17) It may be recalled that in 1968 during the Nigerian Civil War, Britain and its oil companies backed the Federal Government while France and its oil lobbies backed the breakaway Biafran Republic. Going even further, back to early 1963, the tiny West African state of Togo witnessed the murder of its first president, Sylvanus Olympio. The German educated Olympio was outspokenly anti-French but was popular with the Americans, whom he encouraged to invest in his country's mining industry. It turned out that not only did the president's assassin, Gnassingbe Eyadema, enjoy a close relationship with France, but was lavished with lucrative personal loans to smooth his way as the 'big man' of Togolese politics, whilst remaining subservient to France. (18)

Export Credit Agencies

Most of the Western countries have export credit agencies (ECAs), which are government or quasi-government entities whose primary function is to promote exports in risky developing country markets that are considered financially and politically uncertain. ECAs not only provide their home country exporters and banks with loans but also provide guarantees and protection for repayment for private sector loans provided to foreign buyers of national products. ECAs also provide insurance protection for national export against loss if a foreign buyer or other foreign debtor defaults in payment for political or commercial reasons.

In his excellent study of Africa's *Oil Boom and the Poor*, Ian Gary has noted that "In 1998, ECAs- supported export totalled 391 billion US dollars or 8 per cent of total world exports. Export credit agencies have been instrumental backers of extractive industry projects in developing countries, including oil projects in Africa." (19) Generally, ECAs aggressively promote their national corporate interests and, therefore they usually compete heavily with one another in backing projects that will benefit their domestic producers and manufacturers. Gary, (2003:17), has revealed that from 1994 to 1999, 50 ECA projects in Africa, valued at 15 billion dollars, showed that the largest sector was oil field exploration and development. 1 billion dollars were invested in oil exploration alone.

Alongside the over concentration of investment on the extraction of primary commodities is the imperialist countries' relentless drive and pressure on African Governments to privatise – sell off – all their public companies to private, usually, Western companies. We have already noted that one of the cardinal conditions of the structural adjustment programme is the privatisation of public utilities or publicly owned companies. The World Bank, working in conjunction with the donor Governments, bully or cajole African Governments into privatising their public utilities. The UK Government, while claiming to champion the poor in Africa, has relentlessly used its Department for International Development (DFiD) to push privatisation in Africa.

The World Bank and the DFiD use private sector consultant to provide so-called technical assistance. These include organisations and companies such as the UK based, free market obsessed, Adam Smith Institute and Price Waterhouse Cooper, which recorded a total net revenue of US 14.7 billion dollars in the fiscal year of 2003 (20).

Date	Project	Country	Consultant	Contract Value
Aug 2004	Privatisation advisor	Sierra Leone	Price Waterhouse Cooper	£48,820
Oct 2003	Support to water sector regulation	Ghana	Adam Smith Institute	£1,079,100
Aug 2003	De-regulation programme manager	Uganda	Bannock Consultancy	£173,556
Sept 2003	Shareholding divestiture, Zambia National Commercial Bank	Zambia	Price Waterhouse Cooper	£173,203
June 2004	Water, Environment and Sanitation Institutional Assessment	Nigeria	WEDC	£282,104

The case of Tanzania is illustrative. John Hilary tells us that

"As one of the conditions for qualifying for debt relief under the heavily indebted poor countries (HIPC) Facility administered by the World Bank and the IMF, Tanzania was required to engage consultants for the privatisation of the Dares Salaam Water and Sewage Authority (DAWASA). The British company, Severn Trent Water International was appointed as lead advisor to the privatisation which was completed when DAWASA's operations were officially handed over to the UK water multinational, Biwater and Germany's Gauff Engineering in a ceremony on 1 August 2003. Then the so-called Department of International Development paid Adam Smith International £430,000 to mount a campaign promoting the merit of privatisation to unbelieving Tanzanian masses." (21)

John Hilary makes the interesting point about the privatisation process that "by concentrating international support and financial opportunities on the private sector, the preference for privatisation undermines the public sector's capacity at precisely the time when it most needs to be built up. Scaling down the capacity of the public authorities is particularly damaging in remote rural areas, where most new connections need to be made. At the same time, allowing the private sector to pick off the most lucrative urban contracts undermines the possibility of cross-subsidisation within a country's systems, which enable investment in less profitable areas to be offset by the returns from more profitable operations." (Ibid)

Besides the influence of these Western companies and their Governments, African countries have been known to be pressured into appointing ministers who are ideologically sympathetic to the demand of the Western Governments and economic interests. In Nigeria in the 1980s the corrupt regime of General Ibrahim Babangida appointed a former World Bank technocrat as Minister of Economic Development. In fact, Karl Maier (2000) informs us that when Britain's prime minister, Mrs Margaret Thatcher, visited Nigeria in 1988, she suggested that General Babangida exchange his military uniform for civilian clothes and run for presidency. Mrs Thatcher was reported to have said to the General,

"Look, you could get the support of the international community. You are wise, you have the structural adjustment programme, the only thing that is missing is democracy. From what we see, other people have done it before. (22)

Generally the new scramble for Africa is coordinated but coming from different directions. The IMF and World Bank, through their processes, soften up African Governments politically by Aid or financial assistance conditional upon Africa's acceptance of Western policies. Then the Western Governments use their export credit agencies to facilitate private investment in extraction of Africa's primary commodities. There is also the so-called Department of International Development which works hand in hand with such free market obsessed organisations as the Adam Smith Institute, and Price Water House to organise the break up and sell off of profitable public utilities to private foreign companies.

While the West continues to act as if it has exclusive rights over Africa, this assumption of exclusivity is increasingly being challenged by China, whose booming economy requires vast quantities of raw materials such as petroleum oil, copper, zinc and nickel. Like the West, China covets Africa's natural resources. Trade between Africa and China in 2004 was around US$30 billion; in 2005 this rose to US$40 billion and to US$55 billion by 2006. China paid US$2.3 billion for a 45% stake in one of Nigeria's offshore oil fields and promised to invest an additional US$2.25 billion to develop the reserve. China imports 7% of its total petroleum oil from Sudan where it holds 40% stake in the Greater Nile Petroleum Company. In addition, China has invested US$3 billion in refinery and pipeline construction in Sudan. Angola exports 25% of its petroleum oil to China. It is also a recipient of US$2 billion in loans from China in return for supplying 100,000 barrels of oil.

Sanou Mbaye, the Senegalese economist and former member of the African Development Bank, has noted that within a decade, China has overhauled Africa's balance of power, relegating the US and the UK to the third and fourth place, and it is challenging France as Africa's number one economic partner. This has obviously upset the West. The Times newspaper reported that the world's largest Western owned mining companies are turning to the United Nations and the World Bank in an attempt to prevent China from freezing them out of Africa. These companies, such as Anglo America and De Beers, with assets of more than US$700 billion complained about competition from China. These companies plan to use the UN and the World Bank's International Finance Corporation (IFC) to challenge China's operations in Africa.

Whilst China's entry into Africa may not be colonialist or neo-colonialist within the classical definition of these concepts, a critical examination of the pattern of trade reveals a familiar story: Africa is exporting raw material and importing manufactured goods, for which Africans are to blame as they have failed to develop manufacturing themselves. The entry of China in the new "Scramble", may, on the positive side, provide some counter to Western influence in Africa, especially the obviously political strings generally attached to Western aid. China has invested more than US$10 billion to rebuild some of Africa's infrastructure which had collapsed through mismanagement, for example, helping to resuscitate African transport systems. The downside of China's relations with Africa is that the more that Africans become dependent on Chinese financial and technical aid, the more they are likely to succumb to Chinese political influence. There is also the considerable long-term threat to the development of African industries; with the many factors impeding this necessary area of development, a flood of cheap Chinese manufactured goods can only further inhibit the industrialisation needed to spearhead African economic growth.

But blaming the West for all of Africa's problems or lamenting China's growing economic influence does not tell the whole story. Africa's elite collude in the despoliation of African masses. The renewed Scramble for Africa is caused by the failure of leadership in Africa. Who is to blame for the derelict state of Zambian infrastructure or the political thuggery that has become state policy in Zimbabwe? The reality is that Africa's elite collude in the marginalisation and despoliation of African masses. A recent example of such collusion is the New Partnership for Africa's Development (NEPAD).

NEPAD

The New Partnership for Africa's Development (NEPAD) is one of the latest development initiatives established by African leaders to tackle underdevelopment and poverty in Africa. Setting out a vision for a development programme and action plan that is both owned and led by Africans, the authors of NEPAD portray the programme as being anchored to African determination to address the malaise of underdevelopment and the exclusion from the global economy; an agenda set by African peoples through their own initiative and of their own volition, to shape their own destiny.

Published in 2001, NEPAD was led by the South African President Thabo Mbeki, Nigeria's President Olusegun Obasanjo and Algerian President Abdelaziz Boukeflika. However, in the formulation of NEPAD and the shaping of this 'African-led' agenda, these three leaders did not ensure consultation among African civil society, political organisations or other African democratic forces. Extensive consultation did take place but the opinions sought were those of the World Bank, the IMF, trans-national corporations, the European Union and individual Western heads of state. NEPAD is a 'partnership' with Africa's exploiters, requiring African countries to establish and police standards of 'good governance' across the continent in return for increased aid flows, private investment and a lowering of obstacles to Africa's trade with the West (23). As a reward for carrying out policies which dovetail with Western interests, the West has dangled the carrot of extra aid to Africa.

In spite of the rhetoric of self- determined development and an African-led agenda, the African neo-colonial leaders involved in NEPAD remain in the pocket of Western governments and trans-national businesses. The free-market policies espoused in NEPAD will not lead to a transformation of the African economy, as noted by Albert Tevoedjre,

"there is little chance that Africa in its present state of low industrialisation and poor technological capacity will be able to catch up through a greater opening of the markets as suggested by NEPAD and G8. No single theory on international trade has succeeded up until now, in convincingly demonstrating that the opening of markets of developing countries will result in the reduction of inequality and poverty." (24)

It is evident that until Africans demonstrate their collective will for independence, the forces of neo-colonialism that aborted Africa's development will continue to facilitate the new scramble for the continent's natural resource. It is worth exploring the concept of collective will. Manifested by people being united and resolutely determined in defence of or pursuit of a defined objective, the force resulting from collective will can compel opponents to change their course. During the struggle against Apartheid in South Africa, the South African states of Zambia, Tanzania, Zimbabwe, Botswana, Mozambique and Angola formed the frontline states. Despite the economic devastation unleashed by the Apartheid war machine, the frontline states were steadfast in providing bases and support for South Africa's ANC and Namibia's SWAPO.

References

(1)Mkandawire and Soludo, *vii;* 1999
(2)Stigliz, *18;* 2002
(3)Onimode, The Future of Africa, 1992
(4)Bangura, Ysufu, ROAPE, *NO 37, 24- 38;* 1986
(5)Curtis, 102-103; 1998
(6) Stein and Nafziger, structural Adjustment, Human needs and world Bank agena , *Journal of Modern African Studies, 29;* 1991
(7)For details of Western hypocrisy around subsidies, see Farmgate:

the developmental impact of agricultural subsidy, Action Aid, 2002.
See Cultivating Poverty: The impact of the cotton subsidies on Africa,
Oxfam, 2002. See also Ross Hammond , The impact of IMF SAP
policies on Tanzanian Agriculture,1998

(8)ECA/OUA, Opcit, *24;* 1984
(9)Fanta Cheru,Structural Adjustment,primary resources trade and
sustainable development in sub- Saharan Africa , World Development
, No1.22 ,1989.
(10)De Rivero, *92-92;* 2001
(11)Gavarshon, *32;* 1981
(12)Gary, Bottom of the barrel: Africa's oil boom and the poor; 2003
(13)Birmingham and Martin, *30;* 1998
(14)Masden, *236;* 1992
(15)Masden, Opcit, *236;* 1992
(16)Masden, Opcit, *54;* 1992
(17)Gary, Opcit, *16;* 2003
(18)John Hilary, Profiting from poverty, 2004
(19)Hilary, Opcit, 2004
(20) Maier, *64;* 2001
(21)Bond, The NEPAD : An Annotated critique, 2002
(22)Tevoedjre, winning the war against humiliation, *57,* 2002.

Chapter 4

THE ARAB PROBLEM IN AFRICA

Any attempt to understand the sources of mass poverty in Africa would be incomplete without a look at the historic and ongoing role of Arab expansionism in developing and maintaining social and cultural environments that inhibit economic development. Just as European imperialism's access to Africa's resources was underpinned by philosophical justification and reinforced by political and economic structures, Arab expansion into Africa has been facilitated by extensive acculturation. This chapter, offers an analysis of the extent to which Arab expansion is exacerbating poverty in the continent.

In the fifth century an Arab invasion of North Africa began a period of conquest. By the end of 641 AD all of Egypt was in Arab hands, enabling military expeditions into other parts of Northern Africa to be launched as local initiatives. By 709 AD virtually all of North Africa was under the control of the Arab caliphate (1) The acculturation process began with captives of war being either sold into slavery or forced into military service; many nomadic Berbers converted to Islam and assisted the Arab conquerors, replacing tribal practices with new social and political norms. By the twentieth century, when North African countries achieved independence from European empires, most identified exclusively as Arab nations, establishing Arabic as their official language and downplaying the cultural specificity of Berbers, accelerating the existing arabisation process. As Ali Mazuri wrote,

> "The Arab conquest of North Africa in the seventh and eighth centuries initiated the process – Arabisation (through language) and Islamisation (through religion – The spread of Arabic as a native language created new semites, the Arabs of North Africa."(2)

Arab social structures further reinforced the acculturation process, as explained by Ali Mazuri,

> "The process by which the majority of North Africans became Arabised was partly biological and partly cultural. The biological process involved intermarriage and was considerably facilitated by the lineage system of the Arabs. Basically, if the father of a child is an Arab, the child is an Arab regardless of the ethnic or racial origin of the mother." (3)

This has resulted in an almost *de facto* partition of Africa into 'white'

Arab North Africa and 'black Africa' south of the Sahara.

The archetypal example of arabisation in Africa is present in Egypt where the ancient African Egyptian heritage is being appropriated as part of Arab history. The construction of the Aswan dam which flooded and permanently displaced black Africans from their ancestral lands, destroyed priceless artefacts of Nubian origin and gave the impetus to the systematic disfiguring and reshaping of most of the latter-day archaeological discoveries in Egypt. Keen to profit from the souvenir trade associated with the pyramids and the Sphynx, the Egyptian government is in the process of amending its intellectual property laws to include replicas of the ancient relics. A spokesman talked of

> "the necessity of documenting Arab heritage so it would be preserved against plunder and loss" (4)

Cheikh Anta Diop argued,

> "Ancient Egypt was a negro civilisation. The history of Black Africa will remain suspended in mid- air and can not be written correctly until African historians dare to connect it with the history of Egypt. The African historian who evades the problem of Egypt is neither modest, nor objective, nor unruffled; he is ignorant, cowardly and neurotic" (5)

Egypt remains part of the African historical reality, which challenges the narrative of innate African inferiority.

Arab racism, manifested in a sense that the African is innately and culturally inferior to the Arab, appears to be entrenched in the North African states of Egypt, Morocco, Tunisia, Algeria and Libya. In re-naming Egypt, the United Arab Republic, its Arab rulers were clearly stamping an Arab identity onto this centre of ancient African civilisation. When Morocco quit the now defunct Organisation of African Unity in 1984, it aspired to join the European Union. The late president Mobutu Sese Seko once suggested that the North African countries, which pride themselves on their Arab descent, should be excluded from the Organisation of African Unity. In his book, *Themes in Afro-Arab Relations*, Mohamed Omar Beshir noted that,

> "Africa, in many Arab minds, is the Dark continent of swamps and forests, wild animals and diseases. It is not difficult to discern among Arabs, an attitude of superiority towards the African. African civilisation and culture remain a closed book for the educated Arab" (6)

Arab racism also appears to permeate the socio cultural structures of nations such as the Islamic Republic of Mauritania, the Republic of Somalia and the Republic of Sudan. Whilst inter-ethnic clashes are a common feature in Africa, racism exacerbates political turmoil not only in these countries but also spills over in to countries such as Chad and Nigeria. Thus a country such as Sudan has been plagued by civil war stemming from ethnic, religious, and economic conflicts between the mostly Arab population to the north, and mostly Black Africans to the south. Despite being located in one of the harshest environments, Sudan's meagre resources are being deployed on an endless war rather than on socio-economic development. For example, education at the secondary and university levels has been seriously hampered by the requirement that most males perform military service before completing their education. In 2005-6 Sudan's ratio of male enrolment in secondary school was only 35% (UNICEF, UNESCO, including the Education for All 2000 Assessment.

The combination of acculturation and anti-African racism has been evident in the scorched earth military tactics and ethnic cleansing witnessed in the Darfur region of Sudan. However, the enforced imposition of Arab culture and the application of a strict interpretation of Islam on Muslims and non-Muslims alike should not be seen in isolation. These are the methods by which Sudan's northern Arab elite is maintaining its economic and political monopoly, at the expense of civil rights and a fair distribution of the national wealth. Sudan is not the only African country where political expediency and economic interests are clothed in the rhetoric of culture and religion. There have been such conflicts in Ethiopia, Somalia, Eritrea and Chad.

Hundreds of years of cultural domination, political subordination and economic exclusion have had considerable impact on the psyche of the indigenous people of North and North West Africa. There is a significant internalising of the oppression among the descendants of the dark-skinned Moors, the Berbers, and other non-Arab peoples; largely confined to the fringes of North Africa and North West African society, many find it hard to take any vestige of pride in their African heritage.

The African Sudanese poet, S. Anai Kelueljang described the internalised racism of many North Africans in his poem entitled " My cousin Mohamed"

> Listen!
> You Mohammed and I
> Are not brothers,
> You're son of my aunt
> You're my cousin!

Long ago your Arab father came
Also he came with the Holy Koran
And his traditional ways
But without a mistress for a wife

Your father came to live among friends
Not his slaves
For Africans are always generous
And useful friends
until they are offended by despising
Their traditional ways

And then he began to study
The existing tribes and clans
And concluded that the Arab
was culturally and racially superior
To the African man

You are no longer
A pure Arab, like your father
You are the hybrid of Africa
The generous product
Of many years of bloody war
On African land
Your African motherland!

My cousin Mohammed
Thinks he's very clever
With pride
He says he's an African who speaks
Arabic language
Because he has no mother tongue!

Again, he says
It is civilised to speak Arabic!

Among the Arabs
My cousin becomes a militant Arab
A black Arab
Who rejects the definition race
By pigment of one's skin

He says,
If an African speaks Arabic language
He is an Arab!

If an African is culturally Arabised
He is an Arab!

He says
Muslims must know Arabic
Because it is the language of the Holy Koran
And the Holy Koran is the vehicle
For the Arab culture
Because the Arabs are God's chosen people!

My cousin says
The Africans have no culture!
The Africans have no history!
The Africans have no religion!
The Africans have no one language!
The Africans are uncivilised!

He says,
It is his duty to extend
The Arab sphere of influence
Into Africa!

He claims that
Egypt is already Arab!
Libya is already Arab!
Tunisia is already Arab!
Algeria is already Arab!
Morocco is already Arab!
Mauritania is already Arab!
Somalia is already Arab!
Djebuti is already Arab!
Sudan is already Arab!
And soon
Western Sahara shall be Arab
Eritrea shall be Arab
Chad Sahara shall be Arab
And if God's willing
Ethiopia shall be Arab
Let the whole African continent

Become an Arab continent
So that its people can be civilised! (7)

Leaders of indigenous African countries have failed to confront the scourge of Arab racism in Africa. Some of these leaders take the racism for granted or acquiesce in the face of Apartheid-style abuse of human rights in Africa. On the 16 February 1967 in Egypt, Leopold Senghor, then president of Senegal and champion of Negritude said the future of Africa can rest firmly,

> "only on values which are shared by all Africans, and which are permanent. It is precisely this set of values I call Africanicity…Essentially they are cultural values which, as everybody knows, are always conditioned by geography, history and ethnic if not racial factors. I have often defined Africanicity as a symbiosis between the values of Arabism and Negritude. But I have come to prefer the term Arabicity." (8)

Here, Leopold Senghor demonstrated a trait that has characterised African neo-colonial leaders, a lack of any deep knowledge of African society and Africa in all aspects: history, languages, ethnicities and economic potential. Their conclusions about what is best for Africa have therefore lacked clarity and, in many cases, are plainly wrong. How can a leader of Senegal, an important African nation within the African world, talk of 'Arabicity'? What message did it send to Arabs and Africans? Leopold Senghor's misleading analysis played into the hands of the forces of Arab imperialism.

This book explores the Western cultural influence on Africa's neo-colonial elite and, as typified by the example of Leopold Senghor, the Arab cultural influence is also a significant factor contributing to the failure of African leadership to identify with the needs of Africa and its people. However, as highlighted in the earlier section on Sudan, cultural influence serves to reinforce economic interests. Core Arab nations such as Saudi Arabia and Kuwait have used their petro-dollars to entice some African governments into the Arab sphere of Influence. Thus Somalia and Djibouti joined the Arab League while Nigeria, a core African nation joined the Organisation of Islamic Conference.

In addition to securing compliance from African leaders, the petro-dollar plays a significant role in maintaining the political and economic status quo. These economies are structured so that rental income from natural resources and other sources are used to maintain a coercive regime rather than developing the broader economic base and physical infrastructure.

"The state's 'fierce' attributes are reinforced by its rentier status that enables the country's fiscal health to remain disconnected from society's productive economic forces, yet directly linked to the international political economy through its critical hydrocarbon lifeline. The connection between abundant oil rents and the aggrandizement of the authoritarian state cannot be overemphasised" (9)

The political, cultural and economic exclusion of a substantial proportion of the population is key to the survival of these Arab-ruled states in Northern Africa. The expansion of Arab influence into other parts of Africa is a continuing issue, as recently illustrated by Libyan leader Moammar Gadaffi's attempt to create an African 'union government'. The concept was originally proposed by pan-Africanist, Kwame Nkrumah, who led Ghana to independence in 1957, but was challenged by African scholars suspicious of North African Arab interests. Gadaffi, in his new role as chairman of the African Union, is determined to push ahead, rather than depending on the AU reaching a consensus. At the Arab League meeting in 2001 ,Gadaffi declared

" The third of the Arab community living outside Africa should move in with the two – thirds on the continent and join the African Union which is the only space we have "

Gadaffi has also pursued the revival of a Fatimid state, an Islamic Shiite Caliphate that ruled over areas of Morocco, Egypt, and the Levant, from 909 to 1171 AD. This suggests that Arab expansionism in Africa is not a thing of the past but a continuing problem that African people ignore at their peril.

Towards The Re-Africanisation of North Africa

North Africa is geographically and historically African. It has always been inhabited by Africans – Black people in their various shades of Blackness. Like most border nations it has also hosted various immigrant, trading and marauding peoples from across the Northern plains, from ancient Jews, Greeks, Romans and Arabs. Intermarriage between members of the African host community and the predominantly white-skinned settlers has generated a range of shades of skin pigmentation within the modern North African population. Writing during the time of Roman occupation, North African-born St Augustine, was happy to deploy the term "African" when describing fellow citizens, for example,

63

"...one Ponticianus our countryman, as an African, a man in high office in the imperial court." (10)

It is obvious that St Augustine was writing a long time before the Arab invasion and, occupation of North Africa; the arabisation process, as briefly highlighted in this section, has meant that substantial numbers of North Africans would now describe themselves as Arab rather than African.

It is clear that Arab expansionism in Africa has contributed substantially to the continent's economic weakness. Arabisation, reinforced by the family lineage system has led to many Africans self-identifying as Arab. Anti African racism has enabled political, cultural and economic oppression of indigenous Africans, many of who have internalised the racism. African leaders have failed to offer a robust analysis of Arab expansionism and have either subscribed to 'arabicity' or found it in their own interests to accept the status quo. The African spirit of 'live and let live' is a strong value which underpins much of African traditional ways of life. However, Arab expansionism needs to be recognised as having caused substantial damage to the social, political and economic fabric of the continent. It also needs to be seen as a continuing threat to Africa's development in the twenty first century. The challenge for Africans is to find a means of reducing ethnic polarisation and to negate the age-old privilege that is supported by Arab hegemony. It is one of the milestones along the road to African renaissance.

References

(1)see chap. 8 0f the Cambridge history of Africa , by micheal Brett (1978)

(2) Mazrui ,1988 ,p. 90

(3) Mazrui ,1988, p. 90

(4) See Los Angeles Times Blog/Egypt copy right the pyramids? (17/02/08)

(5) Diop , 1974 ,p. xiv

(6)Beshir , 1982 , p. 32

(7)Excerpts from the poem ' My cousin Mohamed), see The myth of freedom and other poems by S. Anai Kelueljang (1985)

(8) Cited in Elenga M'bunyinga ,1982 ,p. 47

(9) Zoubir . Y, et all , 2008 ,p. 12

(10) The Confessions of St Augustine, 193; Hodder Christian classic ed. 1983.

Chapter 5

NIGERIA: AN AFRICAN TRAGEDY

Nigeria gained political independence in 1960. It has a compact land mass extending over 923,763 square kilometres and an estimated population of 120 million. It has the single largest concentration of Africans anywhere in the world. Given its relatively large population and potential market, relatively developed workforce and abundance of national resources, Nigeria was naturally expected to make rapid progress towards industrialisation and economic development; Nigeria has the potential to play a significant role in Africa's struggle for liberation from economic domination but to-date has failed to realise that potential.

Historically, the industrialisation process has tended to involve pioneer nations providing the impetus for economic change across continents. In Europe, Britain was the first industrialised nation, followed by Germany and other European nations. The first Asian nation to industrialise was Japan. Whilst its rampant imperialism was once the scourge of South Asia, Japan provided a model of industrialisation and its investments modernised the economies of other South Asian nations. A transformed Nigeria, Democratic Republic of Congo and South Africa would be powerful forces in this struggle for the industrialisation of Africa and its liberation from economic domination, however only South Africa, with its small industrial base, is able to make even a token challenge to the influx of European and Asian imports.

Since 1970 Nigeria has earned more than US$ 500 billion from petroleum oil alone, which well managed could have eased the process of structural transformation of the economy. Unfortunately the oil monies have not been well managed, as Ian Gary gloomily observed,

"so overwhelming is mismanagement and rent seeking that Nigeria
has unfortunately become virtually synonymous with corruption.
The capture of oil monies is the only big game in town." (1)

In 1977 the Nigerian Federal Government established the Nigerian National Petroleum Corporation (NNPC). NNPC received 57% of all total crude petroleum oil which was then exported, the revenues being deposited in an account at the Central Bank. The monies were stolen by Nigeria's political elite and used for their own purposes, rather than being for transforming the peasant agriculture-based economy to an industrial economy. Nigeria's manufacturing sector is characterised by low productivity and high wastage and has operated at an average of only 30% capacity over the last decade. Between 1997-2003 Nigeria's manufacturing sector has contributed, on average, a meagre 6% to the national output. (2) If light assembly-type manufacture was subtracted, then the contribution of the manufacturing sector is almost zero. It is impossible to go to a market anywhere in the world, including Nigeria, and find an industrial product designed, created or manufactured in Nigeria by Nigerians.

The impact of the mismanagement of the economy is evidenced by the shockingly poor living standards experienced by the majority of Nigerians. Despite its wealth, 70% of Nigeria's population live in absolute poverty. 70% of Nigerians do not have access to clean water and basic sanitation, 65% of Nigerians do not have access to basic medical care. Nigeria's infant mortality rate is one of the highest in the world at 153 per 1000 births. Most Nigerian families live in conditions of abject poverty, a way of life characterised by low calorie intake, lack of access to adequate health facilities, low quality education system, low life expectancy, underemployment and unemployment. Even by African standards, Nigeria's social indices register negatively. (3)

The Poverty of Leadership in Nigeria

In 1970 the Government took the decision to promote industrial production which would be made possible by the oil boom. Amid much fanfare and chest beating, both the federal and state Government launched various 'development' plans which did nothing to kick start economic development and served merely to draw attention away from the enrichment of state officials as they siphoned off national resources, indulging in robbery on a large scale. *

Since 1970 various approaches have been adopted by the Nigerian Government ostensibly to establish the nature and causes of underdevelopment within the country. Each approach has proved ineffectual, both in terms of economic analysis and strategic planning. There has been a tendency to avoid introspection and eschew any meaningful examination of mismanagement or misappropriation within Nigeria's ruling elite and the nation's economic structures.

For example, in 1976 at the first hint of downturn in oil revenues, Nigeria's head of state, General Olusegun Obasanjo, took a loan of nearly £1 billion from private commercial banks in the UK. This was the first of many such loans used to finance a range of projects, many of them "white elephants", resulting in around £2.76 billion being spent during the two years of Obasanjo's regime. (4)

The 1979 Odama Committee, instituted by President Shehu Shagari, preferred to look elsewhere for the causes of Nigeria's economic failure, stating that,

> "one of Nigeria's present economic problems can be regarded as the effect of the world economic recession on the Nigerian economy This world recession gave rise to the oil glut which very adversely affected Nigeria's crude oil sales...our fluctuating economic fortunes in the last decade or so is a pointer to the vulnerability of our mono-economy." (5)

By focusing on the external forces of world oil prices, Shagari was able to justify a structural adjustment programme that incorporated the reduction of public expenditure, privatisation of Government parastatals and companies and imposition of new fees and levies on public services. Whilst articulating plans to diversify revenue sources and achieve self-sufficiency in basic food production through a review of agricultural production, the real intent of the Shagari Government was to borrow from the World Bank and the IMF.

In 1984 President Shagari was overthrown by General Muhammed Buhari, who denounced the Shagari Government for,

> "downright incompetence, irresponsibility, mismanagement, planlessness and half-hearted application of measures designed to curb Nigeria's vulnerability to the vagaries of the oil market." (6)

Although critical of his predecessor, Buhari was unable to develop a progressive economic development programme for Nigeria and the Government planning document of April 1984, The Blue Book, espoused similar economic perspectives as those of the Shagari regime, stressing the need to address national economic deficits through the reduction of expenditure on public services, and criticised the proliferation of the public sector,

> "State Governments presented large budgets ostensibly to impress the electorate. Some Governments budgeted for free education at all levels, free medical services, proliferated the establishment of polytechnics and Universities..." (7)

Buhari suspended negotiations with the IMF and the World Bank, gaining considerable popular support. However he then imposed extremely harsh measures which included stringent fiscal control, mass retrenchment of workers and severe austerity measures. Within 9 months of his arrival in power General Buhari had lost all the goodwill he had garnered for removing the corrupt Government of Shehu Shagari. But more seriously for the Buhari regime, its structural adjustment programme did not go far enough for the International Monetary Fund and Western Governments. Therefore, General Buhari not only lost the goodwill of Nigerians but also he lost the support of the powerful international financial cartels and ultimate spokespeople for Western financial lenders, a mistake his successor was not to repeat.

On 27 August 1985, General Mohammed Buhari was overthrown by his "trusted friend" and comrade in arms, General Ibrahim Babangida. On 12 December 1985, in response to considerable anti-IMF protest from the Nigerian population ,General Babangida announced the termination of an application for an IMF balance of payment loan, and affirmed his fundamental objectives as being, "economic reconstruction, social justice and self-reliance."

However, as with the preceding regimes, such rhetoric merely served to mask the Government's actual intentions. The regime appointed two of Nigeria's leading pro-IMF economists, Dr Chu Okongwu and Kalu Idika Kalu to head the Planning and Finance ministries respectively. Despite the rise of anti-IMF feelings within the Nigerian population, the regime pursued economic policies very much in line with the IMF agenda, relentless stringent fiscal measures and a structural adjustment programme that promoted free-market economics. The full force of this policy was displayed in the 1986 budget, as noted by Yusuf Bangura,

> ".... the Government's 1986 budget pushed the adjustment programme to its logical monetarist conclusion..... The budget was unequivocal in its support for privatisation, removal of subsidies from Petroleum, export promotion, an appropriate market level for the Naira, cuts in salaries and wages and a commitment to future liberalisation." (8)

In 1999 General Olusegun Obasanjo had re-invented himself as a civilian head of state and in April 2000 published "Obasanjo's Economic Direction 1999-2003", outlining his policies for re-structuring Nigeria's economic development and achieving,

> "a strong, virile and broad-based economy with adequate capacity to absorb externally generated shocks. A buoyant economy with a high level of productivity...a national economy that is highly competitive, responsive to incentives, private sector-led, broad-based, diversified, market-oriented and open, but based on internal momentum for its growth..." [emphasis, mine] (9)

Underpinning these ambitious aims were essentially the same old strategies of privatising state-owned industries, increasing oil revenues, promoting free-market economics and negotiating with the IMF and the World Bank. Where the "new and improved" Obasanjo regime seemed to break with tradition was in its declaration of campaign against corruption, starting with an Anti-Corruption Bill. However, the campaign proved to be a red herring, avoiding tackling the issue of corruption at source by characterising the wholesale theft of a nation's resources as being a problem of dishonest individuals rather than a systemic and structural problem rooted in Nigeria's neo-colonial political and economic structures. The recent forced resignation of Nigeria' erstwhile Finance minister, Ngozi Okonjo Iweala, who had been actively pursuing the anti-corruption agenda, clearly demonstrated the lack of serious intent behind Obasanjo's "campaign".

The Nigerian writer Chinua Achebe noted that the trouble with Nigeria is the problem of leadership. As he put it,

> "There is nothing basically wrong with the Nigerian character. There is nothing wrong with the Nigerian land or climate or water or air or anything else. The problem is the unwillingness or inability of its leaders to rise to the responsibility, to the challenge of personal example which are the hallmarks of true leadership." (10)

Achebe could have been writing for the whole of Africa, but his observations raise fundamental questions: What is it about Nigeria – and Africa generally – that militates against the emergence of good leadership? Why is Nigeria struck with a corrupt, vicious and ignorant leadership that reduced the nation to an embarrassment to both African people and the world in general?

Undoubtedly part of the answers to these questions lies in Africa's experience as a colony .. Colonialism engendered an African elite that was dependent and parasitic on their European connection. Out of this elite emerged the post-colonial Government that ruled Nigeria and most of Africa.

At Independence in 1960, Nigeria's political arena was dominated by three major political parties: Northern People's Congress (NPC) in the Northern region; National Convention of Nigerian citizens (NCNC) which derived support mainly in the Eastern region and the Action Group (AG), which was supported mainly by Yorubas in the Western region. These parties were dominated by an alliance of petit bourgeoisie and feudal chief; an alliance that was made up of most of the post-colonial elite, which remained closely aligned to the colonial states in a parasitic relationship.

With the advent of political independence the elite has continued the parasitism of connection with the colonial states and with foreign business. The Nigerian-African elites are not nationalists of the Chinese Maoist or the Russian Stalinist type, who sacrificed personal wealth, interests and pleasures, for a life dedicated to the ruthless pursuit of National Liberation and rapid economic transformation. The Nigerian-African elites are not even capitalist in the sense Max Weber defined it in his book *The Protestant Ethic and the Spirit of Capitalism*

"It is one of the fundamental characteristics of an individualistic capitalistic economy that it is rationalised on the basis of rigorous calculation, directed with foresight and caution toward the economic success which is sought in sharp contrast to the hand-to-mouth existence of the peasant, and to the privileged traditionalism of the guild craftsman ...." (11)

Nigeria's elite and indeed most of Africa's elite are not capitalist in the Anglo Saxon model epitomised by the United States with its emphasis on scientific and technological innovation and creativity allied to aggressive, predatory imperialist foreign policy of sucking in cheap raw material resource from weaker countries.

Nor are the African elite in nations such as Nigeria, Congo, Togo, Kenya, Liberia, Uganda, Ethiopia, Burundi, Rwanda, Sudan, Cameroon, to name a few, capitalist on the Rheinish model of which Germany, Japan and South Korea are known examples, with their emphasis on state-led capitalist development.

The African post-colonial elite have not displayed the characteristics seen in the bourgeoisie of recognised capitalist models because rather than increase their own economic power by stimulating the production of wealth, they have preferred to practice protectionism and theft, inhibiting economic development in the process. As Ake noted,

"This political strategy created an unproductive state capitalism in which surplus was accumulated and distributed with state power and the law of value could not be operationalised. ... Economic success became dependant on State power or State patronage. .... For those who were part of the ruling faction, entrepreneurial activity became unnecessary for wealth could be accumulated faster and with less financial risk by using State power." (12)

Nigeria's post-colonial elite, in common with the rest of Africa, with the exception of Botswana, have shown no creativity, imagination or originality in charting the course of development of the post independent nation-states. In the absence of any meaningful achievement, the only way they maintain their political power and economic privilege is to keep Africa's masses in the condition of endemic poverty.

The Enduring Legacy: Power, Greed and Mediocrity

The history of post-colonial leadership in Nigeria is characterised by greed and mediocrity. Whilst each new regime criticised the previous Government for ineptitude and mismanagement, none has broken away from the vicious circle of incompetence and dishonesty; the faces may have changed but the policies have remained constant. One character has also remained a constant feature, establishing and dismantling the various political regimes, and it is through the prism of his career that the consistency of greed and mediocrity within Nigeria's leadership is best understood.

In January 1966, a clique of Nigerian army officers, primarily of the Ibo ethnic group, overthrew the then civilian government of Abubaka Tafawa Belewa.

In July 1966 a group of young Northern Nigerian army officers struck back with a ferocious vengeance. The Northern army officers led by Theophilus Danjuma and Major Murtala Mohammed attempted to annihilate any Ibo officer within their reach and established Lt Col Yakubu Gowon, a Northern career soldier as Nigeria's Head of State at a time of massive increase in the nation's petroleum wealth. Danjuma took up post as Divisional Commander.

Rather than restructuring and transforming the Nigerian economy from dependence on primary commodities to an industrial one, the Gowon regime showed no inclination for breaking with neo-colonist capitalist relations, perpetuating an economy wholly dependent on foreign technology and industrial products. In July 1975, General Gowon was overthrown by military coup, Col Mohammed became the Head of State, Col. Olusegun Obasanjo his deputy, and Col. Danjuma the Chief of State of the Army.

In July 1976, General Murtala Mohammed, was killed; General Obasanjo assumed the position of Head of State, with General TY Danjuma remaining Chief of Army Staff. Again, until General Obasanjo handed over power to the elected Government of Shehu Shagari, no attempt was made to restructure and transform the Nigerian economy.

Subsequently Nigeria witnessed further coups by General Buhari, 1985, General Babangida, 1986, General Sani Abacha, 1996. Coupists such as Generals Buhari, Babangida, Abacha and others, Generals who bestrode and dominated Nigerian politics may not necessarily owe their careers to General Danjuma but it is arguable that they received the nod and wink from him.This was certainly the case during the coup that removed General Yakubu Gowon from power. Even Obasanjo acquired his positions of Military Head of State of Nigeria in 1976 and civilian President of State in 1999 through General T.Y. Danjuma and his clique, which included General Ibrahim Babangida. This was stated as a matter of fact by General Danjuma in an interview in the Nigerian *Guardian* December 2000. Following Nigeria's return to civilian rule, General   Obasanjo , now President   Obasanjo, became the elected president of Nigeria, and with his friend, General T.Y. Danjuma as the Minister of Defence, Nigeria came full circle

Danjuma's career as "king maker" has been incredibly profitable, enabling him to amass considerable personal wealth. General Danjuma is arguably one of the richest persons in Nigeria. His share in oil companies is currently trading at US$500 million. For example, the London financial newspaper, CITYA.M (Oct, 2005), reported that South Atlantic Petroleum, allegedly owned by General Theophilus Danjuma, has kicked off the sale in London of its US$1 billion stake (£564 million) in an oilfield off the West African coast.

The amassing of considerable personal fortunes has long been the primary aim of the large part of Nigeria's political leaders. The American magazine, National Enquirer (Feb, 1993), revealed that 3000 Nigerian officials have a fortune of US$33 billion in Swiss banks. General Ibrahim Babangida, Nigerian's former dictator, is estimated to have a personal fortune of US$6 billion. The late tyrant and military dictator, General Sani Abacha is estimated to have stolen more than US$2 billion from Nigeria. Following his death, his family in their infinite mercy and grace, handed back US$750 million to the Nigerian Government in 1999. (13)

Nigeria's leadership has completely failed to develop coherent policies and articulate clear objectives against which their success can be assessed. One of Nigeria's most astute political journalists, Tunji Bellow summed up the lack of clear political purpose that has characterised Obasanjo's regime as follows,

> "The ruling People's Democratic Party (PDP) – the party that succeeded the military and controls the Nigerian Federal Government – had no programme ....Because of the lack of clearly identified objectives, the President found himself hijacked by special interests, And because of the absence of well-defined economic policies, the IMF and the World Bank people moved in to overwhelm him." (14).

The fact is that underdevelopment and the phenomenon of mass poverty that characterises Nigeria and the rest of Africa is not a natural condition. Contrary to what growth economists may argue, underdevelopment is not synonymous with poverty and a low level development of productive forces but is directly linked to the relations of appropriation of the society's wealth. . For Nigeria's oligarchy and its collaborators, the prevalence of mass poverty in Nigeria and in Africa generally, is not a failure but the basis of its social, political and economic domination; without mass poverty they would not be rich or wield such enormous power and influence. The oligarchy ruling Nigeria, through the army or via civilian collaborators, does not control political power for the development of the nation.

John Henry Clarke was not overstating the case when he noted,

"...if Nigeria becomes a truly African nation (and not a den of thieves) it can change all of Africa. Half of the lawyers, technicians, African-trained engineers, school teachers and qualified professors in Africa are Nigerians. Nigeria could turn Africa around....but it would have to work as a collective and not as individuals." (15)

References

(1) **Gary,** *27;* 2003
(2) See Obasanjo's Economic Direction,1999 - 2003
(3) See Ali – Akpajiak and Tony Pike ,2003
(4) See the Nigerian Guardian; Jan 9, 1982
(5) The Odama Report, *21 – 50;* 1983. (for a critical analysis of the report
(6) see **Usman,** 1986
(7) **Usman,** *29;* 1986
(8) **Usman,** opcit , *29*
(9) **Yusuf Bangura,** ROAPE,1986
(10) **Obasanjo,** opcit, 2000
(11) **Achebe,** *1;* 1983
(12) **Marx Webber,** *76;* 1930
(13) **Ake,** *15;* 1996
(14) Guardian (UK), 4 October, 2001
(16) **Tunji Bello,** The New Republic; May 14 2003
(17) **JH Clark,** *392-393;* 1994

CHAPTER 6

WAGING WAR AGAINST POVERTY

The greatest obstacle to Africa's social progress and economic development, the ending of mass poverty in the continent, is the ruling neo-colonial elite; where there is no vision, the people perish. As in most other regions of the world, Africa has always had a powerful domestic elite class: tribal chieftains, religious leaders, clan elders and the ruling neo-colonial elite. These domestic interests who constitute the elite, have often allowed their narrow interests to undermine their ability to protect Africa's wider and strategic interest, especially in relation to Africa's rivals and competitors. These powerful interests have often failed, not only to promote the intellectual, political and economic power of African people, but have also all too often collaborated with foreign interests to the detriment of African people. This gives the impression that any race, European, Arab, Asian and Chinese, not only take advantage but also profit easily in dealing with Africans. Rather than provide the appropriate environment and social values that would facilitate the absorption of new ideas and the introduction of changes necessary for rapid socio-economic transformation, Africa's elite have been driven by personal greed, selfish and narrowly conceived national interest. Africa's elite have generally exhibited a disturbing inability or unwillingness to rise to the challenge of personal example which is the hallmark of true leadership. Africa's elite seem to forget that ultimate freedom and independence, as noted by Amos Wilson, in his book, *African-Centred Consciousness versus the New World Order*, is founded on,

> "production, upon the creation of employment, upon the creation of labour and the creation of products for our own consumption, when we look in the world today, we will see that the powerful nations and people are producing people, not consuming people...you can not consume yourself into equality...you cannot consume yourself into power. These nations depending on consumption will see as they consume the product of others and do not produce themselves, that they will be consumed by others." (1)

Students of African history will recall that African middlemen, a powerful domestic interest, supplied slaves and gold to European traders for 200 years. Mackenzie has noted that Africa fulfilled two auxiliary roles in the European scheme,

> "..first as the supplier of Gold to pay for the Asian trade, next as the supplier of slaves for the plantations, cottons, tobacco and sugar of

America." (2)

Thus, wittingly or unwittingly, Africans helped to create a world order that sought to destroy them as an independent political and economic power. During colonialism some sections of the African elite collaborated and even sought the protection of the forces of colonialism. At the time of political independence, political power was transferred largely into the hands of the sections of the elite that would protect and preserve the essential structural legacy of colonialism. The politics of independence and preservation of colonial structures, incisively described by Kwame Nkrumah as neo-colonialism, sucked Africa into a political and economic quagmire from which it is yet to extricate itself.

The State in Africa

Rosovsky (1966) notes that comparative economic history tells us that countries beginning industrialisation in a setting of relative backwardness require leadership and strong action in order to get started. During the period of transition, the private sector and individuals played a less active role; the main emphasis came from the State. (3) Historically, whether capitalist or socialist, the state has always had a very important role to play in getting the process of development started. It could take the form deployed by the British Government in 1699 which banned the import of cotton and woollen cloths from Ireland, and in 1700 the import of cotton cloths from India. Both products were forbidden because they were superior to the British products. As the British industrial revolution was built largely on the textile industry, Britain could , arguably, not have achieved global economic domination without such measures. Elsewhere, in Germany, Japan and most of the rich industrial nations, the State also played a fundamental role in national development. In his magnificent book, *From Third World to First*, the former president of Singapore, Lee Kuan Yew, writes of Park, ex-president of South Korea,

> "Park had been in power for eighteen years and had got the economy thriving with a disciplined and united people, all of whom were determined to achieve economic modernisation. Following Japanese practice, he jealously protected his domestic market and exported aggressively. He encouraged, even forced Koreans to save, denying them luxuries like colour television sets which they were exporting in increasing numbers...Without Park, Korea might never had made it as an industrialised nation." (4)

General Park came to power in Korea at the same time as General Mobutu came to power in the Congo....but the fortunes of the two countries could not have been in sharper contrast.

The State, those who control it and what is done with the immense power of the State is of fundamental importance in understanding the political and economic health of any nation. Since Independence most African states have been controlled by self-absorbed neo-colonial leaders who equate their narrow self interest with national interests.

Ghana, the first African nation to gain political independence and, despite having one of the most dynamic and articulate leaders in Dr Kwame Nkrumah, encapsulated the troubles that were to characterise Africa and which have continued unabated. Whilst Dr Kwame Nkrumah, the first prime minister of Ghana, and a staunch Pan Africanist, was not personally corrupt, his ministers and their lackeys reduced the Ghanaian state to an instrument of their personal accumulation of wealth. Nkrumah's fall was a clear demonstration of the pitfalls facing a leader, however well-intentioned, when surrounded by self-seeking political charlatans and opportunists. Joseph G Amamoo, in his book, *The Ghanaian Revolution*, writes,

"Long before the coup of February 1966 which brought the regime to an end, it was well known that a number of ministers and prominent party officials, who previously were people of modest means at best, or some times, people of rather limited means, had suddenly become not only opulent but also quite corpulent. The dramatic increase in girth, the sprouting of homes and buildings in top areas of Accra, the conspicuous display of affluence and wealth, in a land of poverty and deprivation, could not be explained in any other way but the obvious." (5)

The degeneration of post independence Ghana provoked many scholarly works; one of the most notable was the great African-Caribbean, CLR James, *Nkrumah and Ghana Revolution* (1962). Mr James asked the pertinent question,

"How has all this catastrophe overtaken the people of Ghana? First Nkrumah, like all the other African leaders, has been fooling himself and a lot of other people with dangerous fiction....it is democratic socialism. As long as you don't take it too seriously, as Mr Manley, Sir Grantley Adams, Dr Jagar, Mr Nehru do not take it too seriously, it does no particular harm except to confuse a majority of voters on your behalf. But if like Nkrumah, you do, and Nkrumah is a very serious determined person, you end up with the totalitarian state - no democracy and no socialism....These African countries are backward counties. I know one which is offering any typist, passage, holidays and £3000 per year. The great body of the population is illiterate or semi-illiterate. Their native language is not English or French. That is the language of the Government and the educated. The people for hundreds of years know, have in their bones, the tribal way of life, where the man and his family are responsible for the tribe and the tribe is responsible for the man and his family. They have developed not only a way of life, but a philosophy of life, a way of looking at the world…Now ruling these people are Africans, but Africans dominated by the Western way of life and Western ways of thought….Every step forward creates more and more Westernised Africans, who not only speak Western but live Western, the individual job, the bungalow, the television, the fridge, the trip abroad. In these countries Government controls a substantial part of the economy." (6)

For most African nations, the State has been used largely to facilitate elite consumption rather than production and diversification of the economy or a move away from reliance on primary products. The World Bank has recorded that close to 40% of Africa's private wealth is located abroad. It has been estimated that Africa loses about US$148 billion per year to corruption. (7)

An explanation of the endemic and deteriorating problem of corruption in Africa, and apparent indifference of the African elite, is that from the standpoint of the elite, corruption and mass poverty may not, for them be a failure. For the African elite mass poverty is a pre-requisite for their own accumulation of wealth, their privileges and their social, political and economic domination. Mass poverty is not an original condition, but largely the result of the activities of the African elite and their foreign collaborators. State power is then used to satisfy the material power of the elite rather than pursue a widespread, thorough going programme of economic development, which reaches deeply into the structure of society. Such a thorough going developmental programme would almost certainly sound the death knell for the majority of the parasitic class that rule and ruin Africa. A wide ranging developmental programme would tend to empower the masses, undermining the basis of elite power: extreme poverty, illiteracy, passivity, fatalism and lack of awareness of the outside world. Africa's neo-colonial elite do not seek or desire structural transformation because it threatens the existing class structure, weakening the political and economic foundation of the dominant class. Therefore it is in the interest of the African elite, to adjust, tinker with the status quo and to avoid any meaningful structural change.

Mahmood Mandani has argued that for growth economist relations of appropriation do not exist. He notes that,

"For growth economists underdevelopment is a natural condition, synonymous with poverty and low levels of development of productive forces. They assume the autonomy of the economy, of the technical process of production. And so their solutions for development are all economic and their most advanced formulations are about the rate of saving and investment necessary for industrial take off. However their formulations ignore the fundamental questions of political power and the nature of political decisions." (8)

Thus decisions about what proportion of the national income were to be invested in manufacturing industry or the building of hospitals, roads and schools, or whether such national funds are stolen by the elite, transferred abroad into private accounts or, as is the case with Nigeria, used to build private mansions, buy real estate abroad, import Mercedes Benz cars and luxury Jeeps, are all political decisions. In effect, the question of the nature of investment, rate of investment and whose income is invested in the national category, are all political issues. Would Africa's elite forego the use of their jet-set lifestyle, their private limousines and parasitic entourages that draw on public funds, for a more modest or Spartan lifestyle? Would they be able to curb the nefarious activity of their clientele and minions in their quest for absolute power to support a life of greed, gluttony and debauchery? General Mobutu, former life President of Zaire (Democratic Republic of congo) came to power at the same time as General Park of South Korea. Whilst Park single-mindedly and ruthlessly used the State power to pursue a programme of economic development, transforming South Korea from a backward agricultural country into a rich industrial nation, Mobutu Sese Seko deployed a similar single-minded ruthlessness but to very different ends.

The Koreans, and indeed the Taiwanese and Singaporeans, following the Japanese model, launched into a programme of productivity, growth and economic competitiveness. The State intervened massively to direct the operations of the market, deciding what investments to be made, what sector of the economy to be given priority and even deciding who are in the best position to achieve positive results. General Park forced Koreans to save and denied them consumption of luxuries.

Even making allowance for slight differences in historical circumstances of the South East Asians and Africa, there is a marked contrast between the disciplined approach adopted by the South East Asian leadership and the looting of public resource to fund opulent lifestyles that was commonly practiced by the likes of General Mobutu, General Ibrahim Babangida, General Sani Abacha and the other political opportunists that have disgraced the African political plain. None of these so-called African leaders have made any effort to break Africa's over dependence on primary commodities. Thus after more than thirty years of political independence almost all African nations still rely on those same primary commodities that sustained the economies during colonial times. Given the overwhelming importance of who controls the State and what to do with State power, the fundamental question is what can be done to wrest or transfer power from the neo-colonial elite to those Africans who have the vision and are prepared to work tirelessly and resolutely for African economic development and the ending of mass poverty.

Class Struggle and Social Transformation

Nowhere in Africa has a broad social transformation been pursued systematically. Without embarking on such transformation it is unlikely that there would be any meaningful development. Historically, the ascendancy of one class, or alliance of class, over others through class struggle have often preceded social transformation. Thus the new dominant class would then fashion a new form of development employing its newly won political power to do so. From 1640- 48 England witnessed a revolution that replaced feudal lords with capitalist- landed gentry and the urban middle class. In Meji Japan, the lower class Samurai replaced the old ruling class. Russia (1917) and China (1949) underwent violent revolutions leading to social transformation and industrialisation. Even nations such as South Korea, Taiwan and Singapore, which did not undergo violent revolutions, were deeply influenced by the Japanese and Chinese revolutions. Lee Kuan Yew writes,

"When the PAP government took office in 1959, we set out to have a clean administration. We were sickened by the greed, corruption and decadence of many Asian leaders. Fighters for freedom for their oppressed peoples had become plunderers of their wealth. Their societies slid backward. We were swept up by the wave of revolution in Asia, determined to get rid of colonial rule, but angry at and ashamed of the Asian nationalist leaders whose failure to live up to their ideals had disillusioned us." (9)

Mr Yew continues,

"In England after the War, I met students from China whose burning ambition was to rid China of the corruption and incompetence of the Nationalist Chinese leaders. Hyperinflation and wholesale looting had led to their ignominious defeat and retreat to Taiwan. It was disgust with the venality, greed and immorality of these men that made so many Chinese school students in Singapore pro-Communist. The students saw the communist as exemplars of dedication, sacrifice and selflessness, the revolutionary virtues displayed in the Spartan lives of the Chinese Communist leaders." (10)

Students of South East Asian political economy would broadly agree that the State played a very important role in the process of the creation of surplus extraction and transfer of resource from agriculture to industry. The State in South Korea and Taiwan, for example, had an absolute grip over the agricultural sector, reduced the political power and influence of landlords as a class, changed class relations and established the economic and political conditions favourable to rapid industrialisation. Whilst the South East Asian leaders achieved stability through collective benefit from economic growth driven by productivity and investment, African states tried to achieve stability through employment of government bureaucracy and elite consumption. Thus continued the rule of Africa's neo-colonial elite, a culturally alienated minority, lodged mostly in the unproductive and, often illegal sectors of the economy. They are an international class, thanks to so-called globalisation, who transfer their capital assets swiftly from Africa to the new global markets and off-shore banks. Africa has become an arena for unscrupulous business entrepreneurs seeking quick profits, arms merchants, money launderers and aid workers, many of whom perpetuate the age-old European patronising paternalism towards Africans. African politics is dominated by an elite class that is the human equivalent of the great scavengers of the African plains, vultures and hyenas. Private investment in Africa and South East Asia was broadly at the same levels in 1960-70s. However, total investment in most African countries has declined from 26% of GDP in the 1980s to 22% in 1999. This is in contrast to South East Asia where private investment rates have been around the 82% level (11). Africa has been the subject of countless declarations, international reports by the United Nations, the defunct Organisation of Africa UNITY (OAU), now replaced by African Union (AU). All, as typified by NEPAD, have actually achieved very little. Arguably, because of the chaos and anarchy that is seen to characterise most of Africa's political and economic management, most foreign direct investments has been concentrated in raw material extraction.

Africa's political arena has been the scene of much political violence, civil wars and coups, but no class struggle leading to the transformation of the political system, no structural transformation. Even such relatively   enlightened African leaders as Julius Nyerere (Tanzania), Tserese Khama (Botswana); coupists such as Flt Lt Jerry

Rawlings (Ghana) – who, to his credit, halted Ghana's headlong plunge into total political and economic anarchy, the Stalinist Colonel Mengistu Haile Mirian (Ethiopia), and the radical and charismatic but short-lived Captain Thomas Sankara (Bukina Faso), the only African leader to have declared his personal assets publicly, have been unable to transform their nations, despite their revolutionary rhetoric. These leaders failed to transform the political and economic structures of their society. The balance of power remained in favour of the neo-colonial elite. By the time they had stayed a few years in power, it was business as usual for the neo-colonial elite. Africa's masses are kicked like political footballs by the neo-colonial elite and the predatory forces of international capital. Decisions which affect the lives of Africans are taken without their consultation or approval. The predatory enforcers of international capital take decisions according to their political, strategic and economic needs. Following the devastations caused by the IMF and World Bank policies in Africa during the 1980s, the two organisation changed tack by introducing the The highly indebted poor countries initiative in the 1990s (HIPC).The HIPC Initiative is a scheme to reduce the debt of heavily indebted countries pursuing IMF and World bank supported adjustment programme .To be considered for HIPC assistance, a country must among other things face an unsustainable debt burden and establish a track record of implementing IMF reforms and what it considers sound policies. It is worthy of note that of the 34 countries that received the debt reduction package , 28 of are in Africa. In other words as the 1990s' Structural Adjustment Programmes were falling out of favour and the language of aid began to be centred around the introduction of poverty reduction strategies (PRSP) that did not change the essence of IMF and Borld Bank's policy .Tim Unwin writes :

> "At the heart of the PRSP process is the aspiration of Governments of poor countries to develop unified strategies in collaboration with a diversity of stakeholders, so that their economic and political structures may indeed concentrate on the elimination of poverty." (12)

But what are the 'unified strategies' and who are the stakeholders? Tim Unwin writes,

> "..to the economic agenda of the free-market had been added the political consort of liberal democracy." (13)

This heady mix of mantras, culminated in the Millennium Summit of September 2000, at which the Global Community committed itself to the eight Millennium Development Goals, each with a set of targets to be achieved by 2015. Currently, it is these goals that dominate the rhetoric of global development policy, with the expectation that they will be achieved through the PRSP process and supported by the appropriate allocation of overseas development assistance. In Africa many of the erstwhile neo-colonial elite are making the right noises about democracy, many are re-inventing themselves as would-be saviours and harbingers of a great democratic paradise. Elections are won before any vote is cast . However , it could be argued that the opening up of democratic space , especially if it generates a wider and informed debate, is to be welcomed. But in terms of leadership, what African nations and people need now more than ever, is a political leadership, whose raison d'être is African-centred politics along Pan-African lines, to single-mindedly and relentlessly pursue African economic development. Such leaders will mobilise Africa's masses to pursue a programme of developing industries, raising productivity and ensuring that public institutions function efficiently and are not crippled by corruption and nepotism. Such new leaders will create a domestic productiveness and level of business capacity that encourages entrepreneurialism and patriotism within a well-motivated workforce. Such people-oriented Governments will work with non-Africans where such work dovetails with the development needs of Africa.

Towards a Sustained Economic Development

The term Development means different things to different people but essentially it may be taken to mean growth that is accompanied by significant structural change in production, in economic and political institutions and living standards. For the Nigerian scholar Nnoli, development is first and foremost a phenomenon associated with changes in people's humanity and creative energy, rather than in things. He notes that development is the unending improvement in the capacity of the individual and society to control and manipulate the forces of nature for their own benefits and that of humanity (14). A clear manifestation of this creative energy which has become a symbol of modernity is a sustained economic development entailing structural transformation.

But what is structural transformation? Structural transformation involves a sustained and systematic shift away from traditional low-productivity, primary activities and low-value services to activities that use modern technologies, create new skills, generate exports and employment. Structural transformation invariably entails manufacturing. As Lall and Kraemer-Mbula have noted;

"Manufacturing is critical to changing and modernising Africa's economic structures. It is the main avenue for applying new technology to production and for raising the technical and managerial capabilities. It is crucial to raising and diversifying export, moving the region from its continued dependence upon low value-added and unstable primary products." (15)

Over the last 300 years, through a process of trial and error, Europeans developed and honed their scientific and technological skills, enabling its control of the prevailing global order. In contrast, Africa's stock of scientific skills and technological capacity are the lowest in the world. With skills and capacity comes structural change; that is the application of skill and capacity to initiate fundamental changes both in the way people live and their living standards. As a measure of development, when statisticians talk or write about the number of African families or households that own cars, have access to electricity , telephones and computers; a corresponding question would be how many of these goods and merchandise are created and manufactured in Africa. African leaders have a penchant for white elephant projects - international airports, large stadiums, costly presidential palaces. Most of these projects are built with foreign expertise and materials and sometimes with borrowed money; these projects contribute very little to the production of capital goods. Many Africans who swap the warm vibrancy of the African continent for the depressing, dreary coldness of Europe would readily admit that the lure of a stable political economy and functional infrastructure is what keeps them in Europe. Few will quibble with the proposition that an African manufacturing industry is the key to unlocking the continent's great potential. Not only would Africans be able to manufacture and go some way to satisfying their own needs but the skill and capacity so acquired would also be used to improve the health care system, modernise agriculture, improve communication and upgrade infrastructure.

Since 1960 African nations have invested a lot of resources in education relative to the pre- independence period. In 1989 it was estimated that half a million Africans were enrolled in university. But as De-Walle points out,

"The paradox of a dramatic improvement in individual capacity accompanied an equally dramatic decline in institutional capacity." (16)

The problem then is not so much the inability of the individual African so educated to rise up to the intellectual and physical challenge of the industrialising process but the failure of the State to harness the collective potential of the people into the creative developmental effort. What African people currently need, more than anything else, is radical Pan-Africanist Government which would not only mobilise the masses, increase the absolute scale of accumulation by curtailing the luxury consumption of the African elite but also alleviate the suffering of the masses. But the neo-colonial interest that controls the State make it impossible for Africans to put their creativity, initiative and knowledge into practical use.

About two years ago, on my way to Lagos, I sat in the plane with an English turbine engineer. He had been called upon to repair some of the turbines that supply electricity to the city of Lagos. He informed me that he did not know why he had to be called out to Nigeria when the job could well be done by Nigerians themselves. He indicated that all he would be doing was to supervise what the Nigerian workers were doing and added that economically his trip did not make sense. However, from the perspective of a typical Nigerian business man or contractor it makes perfect sense to bring in a British engineer. Firstly, they can charge more for the foreign expert. Secondly, it is probably that the Nigerian contractor has a hotel and so would be able to build in expat rates into the contract cost. If during the Nigerian Civil War, the break-away Republic of Biafra built its airport and mobile refinery to support its war effort, why has Nigeria and the rest of Africa failed to harness the skill and capacity of Africans? A possible answer is the politics of Neo-colonialism. De-Walle has argued that

> "after four decades of independence and tens of billions of dollars in state capacity projects, low state capacity in Africa cannot be viewed as the unfortunate, if inevitable by-product of underdevelopment. It should instead be perceived as the direct consequence of formal policies and informal practices of Governments for which a developmental state apparatus is not a high priority." (17)

Sustainable development

The World Commission on Environment and Development (WCED), 1987, otherwise known as the Brundtland Commission, defined Sustainable Development as that which meets the needs of the present without compromising the ability of the future generation to meet their own needs. For Rackalshaws (1989) Sustainable Development is the emerging doctrine that economic growth and development must take place and be maintained over time, within limits set by ecology, the biosphere, and the physical and chemical laws that govern it. Sustainable Development is applicable to issues as varied as industrial and urban development, technology, agriculture, energy, architecture and the environment. Sustainable Development envisages changes in thinking about what constitutes 'Development' and raises questions about orthodox development with its narrow emphasis on growth versus erosion of autonomy of local communities, the using up of local resources and the creation of long term dependence. Sustainable development is particularly relevant to Africa as it grapples not only with the challenge of transforming the economy from one based on primary products to one based on industry, but a formidable problem in the encroaching Sahara Desert. Countries such as Niger, Sudan, Mauritania, Chad, Ethiopia, Somalia and Northern Kenya are arid and fragile; they are plagued by the scourge of drought. Peasants who could previously feed their families are not able to do so because of the drought; the struggle to eke out a living in a harsh terrain has been compounded by droughts, making both arable and pastoral farming an extremely difficult, if not hopeless task. What is needed is a concerted effort by the people, a people-orientated Government and a massive mobilisation of Africa's human and material resource, channelling the efforts into industrialisation.

Aid and Development

Few states in the world would claim not to have received aid in one form or the other. The Jewish state of Israel, for example, occupies an arid land, and was narrowly focused on agriculture. But 50 years on, Israel has been transformed into the Silicon Valley of the Middle East. The Jewish state is a recipient of American Aid, in the region of US$1.7 billion dollars annually and is also the recipient of about US$500 million dollars of private funding annually from the Jewish Diaspora. Israel's per capita income is about US$16,850. After the Second World War, Europe was also the recipient of American Aid to rebuild its shattered economies. Africa, as many European analysts never tire of telling anyone who cares to listen, has been a major recipient of Aid. De-Walle, for instance has written,

> "It has long been fashionable in certain circles to advocate a 'Marshall Plan' for Africa to spur economic growth, but in fact Africa's dismal performance has come in the context of a substantial flow of Aid resource to the region. The donors responded to the onset of the debt crisis in Africa with a substantial increase in aid....As a result, Africa received 24 per cent of total official development assistance (ODA) in 1980 but some 37 per cent in 1993" (18)

Similarly, Matthew Lockwood, in his aptly titled book, *The State They're In, An Agenda for International Action on Poverty in Africa*, writes,

"Sub-Saharan Africa received US$23 billion in official aid in 2003...Africa has received aid over a much longer period of time..." (19)

But much of the Aid flowing into Africa is like a series of mis-directed arrows; many Aid projects miss their proposed targets. For Africa's neo-colonial elite having failed to manage Africa's resource wisely, foreign aid is simply more resource to mismanage. Some, like Mobutu, could not believe their luck and pocketed as much as they could.

Two major factors have often undermined the effectiveness of Aid to Africa: corruption and poor governance of the African countries and the hypocrisy of the donor communities, earlier referred to as Western Rhetorical Ethics (Chapter 1 Page 5) Studies have shown that of the total official Development Aid of US$69 billion in 2003, only US$27 billion was real Aid. In other words 61 per cent was Phantom Aid; that is Aid, for example, counted as debt relief, over priced and ineffective technical assistance or money spent on excess administrative cost . A big difference exists between official Aid declarations of the donor countries and the actual aid received by the recipient states. In 2003 the western industrialised countries' official Overseas Development Aid was US$50 billion but the total actual Aid received by the recipient developing countries was US$16 billion. Studies have shown that countries such as US, France, UK and Japan, in spite of their rhetoric, do little to help the poor of Africa. (20)

70 per cent of US and Italian Aid, excluding food Aid and technical assistance, is tied to the purchase of their goods and services. France spends US$2 billion of its Aid budget each year on technical assistance, including the maintenance of the private jet of President Omar Bongo of Gabon, and US$0.5 billion on refugees and immigration expenditure. Official Aid is used to pressure and dictate what policies African Government should implement with strings attached, it is wasteful and has corrupting impact. Thus Meles Zenawi, the president of Ethiopia complained in 2000,

"The various conditionalities introduced have not only slowed down the process, but have further undermined the capacities and functions of state institutions." (21)

But the fact is that Africa has lost in the region of US$285 billion to the West between1970-1996.

The West plays host to an array of organisations that are labelled charities, some of which, for example Action Aid and Oxfam, do good work in their commitment to exposing the hypocrisy of Western governments. But the Aid industry also spews scavengers who, both in terms of the needs of their own personal egos and business interests, live off the suffering of Africans. Bob Geldof, for instance, meant well when in 1984 he focused the world's attention to the catastrophic famine that engulfed Ethiopia. But since then, not only has he allotted to himself the role of Africa's spokesperson, it has also become apparent that he has become a weapon in the armoury of the West's Rhetorical Ethics, delivering misinformation about the West's political and economic relationship with Africa. The Live-8 event that he organised in 2005, ostensibly to draw attention to poverty in Africa, created a cultural apartheid, excluding African musicians on the basis that they had not sold more than the pre-requisite 4 million records established as the criteria by which an artist was judged worthy of inviting to perform. In addition, Geldof's Live 8 event was sponsored by the very transnational corporations whose activities are blighting the lives of millions in Africa, namely Nestle, BAE Systems and Rio Tinto

As stated by the New Internationalist,

> "..as the enormity of his fame after Live Aid hit home, Geldof left the Boomtown Rats to launch a solo career and to release his autobiography...In 1992 he co-founded Planet 24...in 1994 Geldof sold Planet 24 to Carlton TV, netting an estimated 7 million dollars...He launched two new ventures: an online travel business, which he sold in 2001 for an estimated overall package of US$17 million...Geldof's phenomenal success as a venture capitalist has led him to see Africa's salvation in his own image. Although part of the Make Poverty History campaign, his political closeness to world leaders saw him front Tony Blair's Commission for Africa...with its emphasis on public-private partnership, free trade and foreign direct investment." (22)

The clear endorsement of the West's imposition of its neo-liberal model of development on Africa, free trade, foreign direct investment, and continuing privatisation of Africa's public utilities could not have been anything but a propaganda coup for the forces of neo-colonialism. As if a Bob Geldof were not enough, another would-be saviour of Africa has emerged to parade himself – the U2 band singer, Bono. If these people have plenty of money to give to charities they would be better to do so quietly and secretly.

References

(1) Amos Wilson, *page 55;* 1999
(2) J Mackenzie, opcit, 5; 1983
(3) Rosovsky, *14-15;* 1966
(4) Lee Kuan Yee, *532;* 2000
(5)JG Amamoo, *32;* 1988
(6) CLR James, *181-182;* 1962
(7) Lockwood, *63;* 2005
(8) Mahmood Mandani, 5; 1982
(9) Lee Kuan Yew, opcit, 496; 2000
(10) Lee Kuan Yew, opcit, 496; 2000
(11) Lockwood,opcitt ,p.86
(12) See Tim Unwin, TWR ,1501 – 1523 ,2004
(13) See Tim Unwin , opcitt ,2004
(14) Nnoli,p.36,1981
(15) Lall ,4 ,2005
(16) De – Walle 133, 1999
(17) De –Walle , opcitt ,133
(18) De – Walle ,p.7 ,1999
(19) Lockwood ,p.15 ,2005
(20) Real Aid : An agenda for making Aid work (Action Aid ,2005) see page 17-28
(21) New internationalist , Jan/feb 2006

Chapter 7

THE WAGES OF FAILURE

The previous chapters of this book have illustrated the ways in which the lack of a unified response to the threats of European imperialism and Arab expansionism has had serious political and economic consequences for the structural development of Africa. The book has also looked at how the lack of a coherent and principled leadership has prevented the development of African economic models to counter the damaging liberal free market hegemony. Running through the book's illustrations and analyses there has been the interlinking and mutually reinforcing themes of the psychological damage at the individual level and the economic impact of consistent and collective failure.

My people, of Obukegi village in Nigeria, have a saying, that the wages of failure is daily humiliation. As general rule Obukegi people will brand a failure a man who cannot cultivate enough farmland to feed his children, provide shelter for his family and above all defend his family's farmland. For the people of Obukegi begging is a sign of failure and weakness, and to be branded a failure is to wear the badge of weakness. A person so branded becomes an object of charity , derision and contempt. Living at the mercy of others, appealing mainly to their conscience a man deemed a failure would lose his right to self-respect and consultation on the making of major decisions within the village. The experience of Black people over the last three hundred years attests to this: Weakness and equality do not mix.

A fictional account of the social and psychological effect of failure and weakness is the story of Mr Unoka in Chinua Achebe's, *Things Fall Apart*. Unoka was always in debt and his kinsmen at Umuofia not only saw him as a failure but were embarrassed by him. Okonkwo, the hero of *Things Fall Apart*, and the son of Unoka spent the rest of his life trying to expunge from himself any sign of failure and weakness. This led ultimately to Okonkwo's tragic death. A not too dissimilar case is the biblical story of the struggle between Goliath and David. It is instructive that few people within the Christian world are called Goliath, in contrast to the near universal use of the name David. It will be recalled that Goliath's tragedy was that he lost a battle to David in a most humiliating circumstance; Goliath was a giant of awesome power and reputation, he was out-thought and out-fought by David. While David's name became associated with imagination, inspiration and ultimately success, Goliath's name has forever been tarnished by the failure and humiliation he suffered at the hands of the young upstart, David.

On a broader level, history centres on achievement; those who are perceived as non-achievers are relegated to the bottom of the scale whether on a personal or a collective level. It is clearly a misrepresentation of the facts to suggest that Africans never achieved anything and the debate continues *(see eg Stephen Howe(1998); Martin Bernell(1987).* But the reality today is that Africa is the poorest continent in the world. (2) Not only has Africa continued to lack the material strength to guarantee its territorial integrity and ability to preserve its autonomy to take decisions in the political, economic and cultural field, but also Africa's material inferiority continues to place the welfare and future of African people at the mercy of non-Africans. Amartya Sen, in his foreword to a report of the Independent Commission on Africa and the challenges of the third millennium, notes that,

> "historical accounts give us a very different picture of Africa in the early centuries of the last millennium. There were, to be sure, many variations, and there were certainly no unity, nor any over arching vision of an integrated African civilisation. Rather, the diverse cultures that made up the continent stood on their own ground and defended their respective ways; there was no general lack of self-confidence that would characterise Africa some centuries later." (3)

It speaks volumes, that after more than thirty years of African political independence, the British prime minister, Tony Blair could, in the contrived emotional terms required to generate good media headlines, proclaim Africa to be, *"..a scar on the conscience of humanity."*

The absence of an appropriate response from African leaders is a symptom of Africa's failure to wrest its destiny into its own hands. It is also symptomatic of the failure of 'white' men and women to rise above the type of politics which subordinates everything to the pursuits of the West's narrow nationalist interests; the type of politics that spawned the self - centred development model that seeks to promote the economic needs of the West above those of the majority of ordinary people whether they live in Africa, India or South America. Tony Blair could have been echoing an earlier speech of King Leopold of Belgium who, while he robbed and murdered the people of Congo, declared his intention to,

> "..open to civilisation the only part of our globe which it has not yet penetrated, to pierce the darkness, which hangs over entire peoples, is, I dare say, a crusade worthy of this century of progress." (5)

90

Despite most African nations having achieved political independence but as Carter Woodson observed,

> "No systematic effort toward change has been made possible, for, taught the same economics, history, philosophy, literature and religion which have established the present code of morals, the Negro's mind has been brought under the control of his oppressor. The problem of holding the Negro-Blackman - down, therefore is easily solved. When you control a man's thinking you do not have to worry about his actions. You do not have to tell him to stand here or go yonder. He will find his 'proper place' and will stay in it."(pxiii) (6)

Having lost economic and political power in relation to other races, especially Europe, African people adjust economically, politically and culturally to agendas set by others; the loss of autonomy makes African people easy prey to the economic and political machinations of Africa's rivals and detractors. Even in cultural forms, such as music, where African people's creative achievements have defied suppression, it is still controlled by others; no African country has the ability to manufacture and disseminate music using the latest technology.

The Psychological Impact of the Humiliation of Africans

The economic, technological and political weakness of Africans, impacts upon African people differently, depending upon where they live. For many Africans who live on the continent, there is the obvious and ever present scourge of debilitating poverty, the masses of people wasting away in destitution and penury. A more important, but less talked about issue is that the failure and the weakness of African people has created a condition of internal racism within Africa. As already noted in Chapter 4, there is a notable issue of Arab anti-African racism in North Africa where Black African people are considered inferior slaves. Muammar Gaddafi, arguably one of the most radical political leaders to have emerged from North Africa, calls Libya 'Arab' Jamahiriya. Gaddafi has, consistently been critical of Western imperialism but not of Arab imperialism. The impact of the potent force of Arab culture has caused many North Africans to internalise the racism, feeling that their African race does not measure up to the standards of other people, Arabs in particular.

For Africans in the diaspora, whose great grand parents suffered the indignity and humiliation of forced emigration in chains, the failure of Africa to control its political and economic destiny is a burden, a challenge to their collective humanity in a hostile world. There has been a considerable impact upon the psyche of African people resulting in many within the Caribbean and South America playing down their Blackness. The Great African American historian, John Henrik Clarke in 'Who Betrayed The African World Revolution' notes,

"Caribbean people in general, both at home and abroad, though they deny this with voices like thunder, are in retreat from their blackness. Most of them are quick to tell you about their English blood, their Scottish blood, without reference to their basic blood which is African. Too many times they are not only divided along colour lines, they are divided along gradation of colour....Though the Caribbean people created a clear revolutionary heritage in the fight against the brutality of slavery...however, presently too many Caribbean people still act as though slavery did not occur in the Caribbean islands at all.. (7)

This collective cultural trauma within the African Diaspora continues to have social and economic consequences. For example, in the UK, statistics show that 30% of African Caribbean men are married to white European women compared to a 2% interracial marriage rate in the overall population (Office for National Statistics 2001). These comparatively high levels of inter-racial marriage between African Caribbean men and white women could indicate an underlying disconnectedness between men and women within the African Caribbean community. Additionally single-parent households, mainly headed by single mothers, constitute 42% of all African Caribbean "family" households in Britain (Source Canadian Journal of Latin American and Caribbean Studies, Jan-July, 2004) This is compared to a UK average lone parent household rate of 25.58% (Office for National Statistics 2004). Whilst lone parenting does not necessarily equate to dysfunctional families, there is clear evidence across a range of indicators to suggest that by disproportionately practising this family model, the African Caribbean population is considerably limiting its potential for socio-economic success.

The extent to which Africans in the diaspora reconcile themselves to their African-ness; the degree to which they look to the African continent as a source of identity, as a cultural reference and as an economic resource, falls far short of the ideal. Peter Wade (1997) could have been expressing the wages of failure of Africans in his eloquent description of the tendency for successful Black people to move away from other Black people as they progress socially and economically,

"... Often, even if they have no personal motive to whiten themselves or their children they are absorbed into a non-black social matrix, thus reiterating the hierarchies of the racial order. On the other hand, non blacks continue to control most economic opportunities and blacks who are not successful are marginalised...forming cultural and physical nuclei of blackness which again seem to reiterate national hierarchies by associating blackness with poverty..." (p86) (8)

The lack of unity between the Africans in the diaspora and Africans on the continent is nothing short of tragic, when a sense of common purpose could do so much to alleviate the conditions of all Africans.

The Falsification of African Consciousness

Amos Wilson wrote that the character of individual and collective consciousness and the range of their behavioural possibilities are significantly influenced by the quality of their recording and recollections of their historical experiences. For Africans living through economic decline and political deterioration, a lack of positive references can have a significant detrimental impact upon their ability to look forward and plan for the future. Force of mind, a sense of group identity and the ability to draw upon individual and a collective sense of worth in this context may be abbreviated to 'consciousness'. Widespread intellectual, emotional and political defeatism amongst Africans is the legacy of generations of poor leadership and negative external influences. Amos Wilson observed,

"To manipulate consciousness is to manipulate possibilities; and to manipulate possibilities is to manipulate power." (Wilson, 1993, pp1-2) (9)

Manipulated or stunted consciousness is severely limiting the ability of Africans to address their economic, political and social development. In order to understand the power of this as a mechanism to encourage the weak to reinforce power structures it is worth looking at some examples of its usage throughout history.

Martin Bernal, in his *Black Athena*, records senior Ancient Egypt condemning Ancient Greeks in the *words*, "Your Greeks are always children." (Martin Bernal, 1987, p107) (10)

The Jews, in accordance with the Bible's Old Testament, declared themselves God's chosen people. This doctrine in no small measure aided the Jewish exodus from the Ancient Egypt of the Pharaohs. Similarly, the unifying mantle of Islam enabled small, often warring

Arab tribes, to expand their power and influence across the world.

In its imperialist phase European nationalism was well served by the artificial construct of 'whiteness' to denote Europeans, appropriating Christian iconography and Hindu racism, making everything black bad and anything white good. This sense of superiority, once allied to economic and technological power, underpinned the worst excess of European colonialism and racism. Whilst European skin colour is generally pink and not white as claimed, as an abstract expression of European nationalism, 'whiteness' was an extremely effective ideological tool, enabling skin colour to be the determinant of ranking within a racial hierarchy; the further away from the abstract construction of whiteness, the less the humanity. Whiteness, the highest representation of European nationalism, rests upon the continued political, economic and technological domination of the Globe by Europeans. Once this is understood, it then becomes clear why technological and military superiority underpin European power. It is also , arguably , an explanation for the United States' annual expenditure of over six hundred billion dollars on weaponry, rising to seven hundred billion dollars in 2008 (*Center for Arms Control and Non Proliferation, Feb 2008*)

Many European commentators, writers and manufacturers of public opinion have imposed artificial determination upon Africans. Thus references are usually made to Black Africa. Richard Buckley (1997) produced an edition of his *Understanding Global Issues* titled Black Africa. But then he has only deployed a phrase which is in common usage. Who then are White Africans? Chancellor Williams (1987) confronted this problem as he asks,"How did all-black Egypt become all white Egypt?" (p18) (11)

He went on to note that,

> "white Africanist writers always concentrate on the "ethnic differences" amongst Africans, the tribal "antagonisms", the "hopeless" language barriers, the cultural varieties etc, they even make separate "ethnic" groups of their own mulatto offspring from slave women by classifying them "white" in some areas and "coloured" in others. Hence a system of thought and practices was developed." (p21) (12)

As most North Africans would not be classified as white in any European country, it would seem that its usage in Africa is an instrument to divide and rule: rich progressive white European versus poor, backward black African.

Today the pervasiveness of religion and the role of African pastors and imams serves to reinforce the rejection of African identity and culture, the obliteration of the historical consciousness. John Henrik Clarke noted,

"The most effective and most tragic of all the European colonisation schemes is the colonisation of the image of God. When you destroy a people's self-confidence and their concept and of image of God as they conceive him to be, it is not necessary to build prisons to contain them because psychologically you already have them in prison." (16)

For those struggling to visualise a fully economically developed Africa, it is worth noting the words of John Henry Clarke,

"European domination has nothing to do with the European having a superior mind, of having ability that you (Africans) do not have. It has to do with the fact that the European believed he could do it and gained enough confidence to do it. We (Africans) can do the same if we make up our minds to do it." (13)

The Future of African People

One of the central themes of this work is that African political and economic weakness, the chronic poverty that afflicts the continent, is due primarily to lack of the production of goods. This section is concerned specifically with the application of science and technology in production needed to achieve industrialisation. Survival in the Global economy necessitates production based on science and technology.

Political power and economic welfare are founded on production; it creates products for consumption, generates employment and fosters the development of skills. Most powerful nations produce more than they consume. Britain's global power was facilitated through its productive power, becoming the work shop of the world. The United States developed from humble beginnings as a nation of European immigrants and enslaved Africans into an economic and political giant through industrialised production. Germany, Japan, the Asian tigers and, more recently, China, are powerful mainly because of their production and the export of goods. Industrial nations producing goods which are demanded all over the world, are those best equipped for survival in the highly competitive Global Economy.

Africa's relegation to what in international politics is classified as the 'Third World' is largely due to its glaring lack of scientific and technological production. Despite Africa's enormous resources which, with proper management and development could catalyse considerable economic growth, most African leaders accept the continent's position as 'Third World' and shamelessly rattle their begging bowls for aid. As discussed earlier in this book, aid cannot be viewed as Western altruism since Western leaders are not elected to look after the interests of Africans. Africa's salvation lies in rapid industrialisation and production.

Africa cannot elevate itself from the category of 'Third World' by consuming other people's products. There is a clear need for a functional and productive economy but to achieve this will necessitate structural, cultural and political change. Africa's leadership will need to be comprised of those with a focus on developing the continent's productive capacity; they will need to be very different from the current cadre of leaders focused on enjoying the fruits of other people's creativity and production. Dedicated, modest, honest and well-informed, the new breed of leaders will need to submerge themselves in the service of African people, demonstrate an abhorrence of greed and detestation of vanity. Leading with humanity and integrity such leadership will need to create the conditions that engender a broad-based mass participation in industrial expansion, linked to extensive but good quality education and good healthcare. Above all, a concerted effort must be made to liberate Africa's rural housewives, peasant women whose suffering and exploitation has grown under the self-indulgency and neglect of African leadership. The economic exclusion of these women is a considerable wasted resource and as mothers, they have significant influence on future generations.

The challenge to industrialise, to improve production and create a vibrant economy will necessarily involve the modernisation of traditional African culture. Whilst culture is the foundation upon which a people rest, it should not become a dead weight that drags down society. Like most other cultures, there are aspects of African culture that are obscurantist; certain traditional African practices, such as female circumcision and necromancy. Such defects are as deplorable as the stoning of women for adultery in Arab culture and the immolation of widows in Indian culture. Traditional African culture suffers from the urban/rural dichotomy; the association of the urban with modernity and rural with backwardness and the primitive. Without modernisation, culture presents a significant obstacle to Africa's will to achieve real independence and development; there is a need to bring together the best elements of each and discard those ways of thinking and cultural practices which hinder socio-economic and political development.

The history of Africa's economic, political and cultural oppression in the service of European and Arab economic interests could be interpreted as a demonstration and justification of Social Darwinist philosophies; if the rule is dominate or be dominated then the gain of one group must by necessity mean the loss of another group. However, such reductionism is both politically unsound and defeatist. Far better for African states to plan how to engage effectively with the global economy in order to participate as a equal partners in the spirit of the African traditional world view of Live and Let Live, expressed in the traditional Igbo proverb,

> "Let the eagle perch, and let the kite perch,
> which one that denies the other its rightful position should lose its wings."

THE ROAD TO RENAISSANCE

The fundamental challenge facing African people both in Africa and the diaspora is how to respond to the economic challenges of the 21st century in order to move beyond survival and achieve an African Renaissance. This will necessitate three major revolutions: revolution in the African mindset/thinking, revolution in skills, and revolution in values. These three revolutions are interlinked but will be dealt with separately for greater clarity.

Revolution in Mindset

Centuries of political and economic impotence have not created the optimum conditions for a 'can do' culture. Achieving African renaissance will require the ability to see beyond the Aid and Aids narrative, whereby the African is helpless and needing help from an external benefactor. It will also require a willingness to tackle a self-interested leadership and endemic corruption. Most importantly it will require clarity of vision and a well considered implementation plan for wholesale structural economic change across the continent. Such an approach, well thought-out, clearly articulated and effectively delivered would create a virtuous circle of sound economies which create the conditions for growth which in turn fosters the innovative thinking needed to create sound economies.

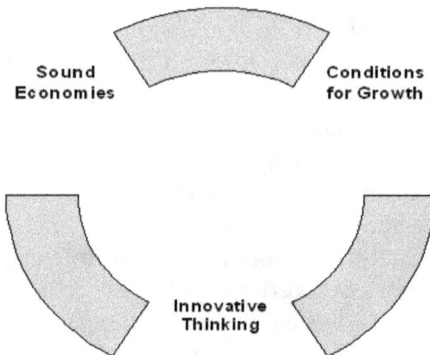

Sound Economies — Conditions for Growth — Innovative Thinking

Revolution in Skills

Delivering an African Renaissance will require a dramatic up-skilling of Africa's workforce. Moving away from primary production to an economy focused on higher value-add activity will require a significant programme of education and training; Africa's stock of scientific and technological skills, in particular, is the lowest in the world.

The Ogba clan of Nigeria have a proverb that a wise father teaches his children to do things for themselves, rather than expect other people to do it for them. If only Africa's leaders could observe this simple truth. Any model of political economy that is adapted and operated in Africa which does not create the conditions for the development of indigenous scientific and technological skill is a bankrupt system and a complete waste of time for the African masses. The failure of Africa's elite to prioritise the knowledge and skills agenda has resulted in 'dependent modernisation' whereby most of the modern technology used in Africa is made elsewhere.

Since independence, Africa's leaders have deluded the masses with the notion of the transfer of technology, the idea that benevolent Westerners and their multinational companies will transfer skills and knowledge to the African. This obviously has not happened and in the meantime, the cumulative process of acquiring technological and scientific skills has barely begun. It is vital that Africans begin the process of learning through trial and error, for this is Africa's primary route to a serious indigenisation programme of action to develop the skills to overcome underdevelopment. Currently the emphasis is on the orthodox technology paradigm which sees the process of technological development as proceeding from the laboratory, followed by adaptive development and then diffusion through the market. However, this is an approach that suits the industrialised nations but is not suitable for African countries which lack the research capital present in Western multinationals, the specialist skills within the workforce, and the global reach which enables maximum market diffusion to recoup research investment and to achieve considerable profit.

Firstly African states must reduce and control very tightly the elite consumption of imported luxuries and the exporting of capital to the money laundry outside the continent. As far as Africa's masses are concerned, that is money poured down the drain. But more importantly the state must invest and be actively involved in the development of a productive manufacturing industry. African engineers must be fully involved in the development of products such as bicycles, motorbikes, basic electrical goods, including the use of solar energy. African

engineers must be used to construct drainage systems, bridges and pipe-borne water. The completion of a project or product cycle would not only enhance the capacity to manage production actively but would also provide Africans with the skills and knowledge to initiate, to manage and to generate technical change. (11) During this incubation period, people would be given the opportunity to explore their creative ability, expressed in the challenge of production. Most of the developed nations and the newly industrialised countries had such a period of incubation. For African nations during this time there would not necessarily be a complete exclusion of foreign investment or trans-national operations. There would not be a requirement for complete autarky, however the involvement of external companies should only complement the national domestic effort; a time would come when the development of the national economy and the skill levels of the people would be such that orthodox free market competition would be a viable option. China is going through that process currently. This issue is also the subject of the John Galbraith book, *The New Industrial State*. But tackling skills development in Africa is faced with a major problem, that of public sector inefficiency in Africa. As a UN study noted,

" .. the public sector was not able to perform its function effectively because of its accumulation of excessive power, lack of accountability and representation, indifference towards public needs and demands, official secrecy and inaccessibility ,and role in depoliticizing the public sphere." (20)

The inefficient and corrupt nature of the public sector would severely inhibit the planning and implementation of such an ambitious and wide-reaching scheme, which would require robust sector analysis and skills profiling, transparent systems for the mobilisation and disbursement of funds, and reliable evaluation frameworks. The revolution in skills could not therefore be achieved without a corresponding revolution in values.

Revolution in Values

African renaissance requires a revolution in values. Traditional African values are anchored in a communal, collective and co-operative system, which as general rule rested upon a strong ethical and moral foundation. There are traditional festivals with the same cultural significance as Christmas for Christians and *Eid* for Moslem. For Ogba elders pouring libation involved, calling on the guardians deities and ancestors as witnesses, that if ever they had denied anyone opportunities for self-fulfilment, corruptly enriched themselves, stolen, or killed, that the wrath of the deities and ancestors should be visited upon them and their family. Consequently the power and authority of the clan elders was based not so much on grounds of personal wealth but on perceived and assumed sound moral and ethical grounds. Peasants could place their faith on the governance of the elders in the full believe that their leadership was transparently honest, scrupulously trustworthy and had the best interests of the community at heart. These communities may not been a moral paradise, but to some varying degrees, there is a traditional African moral value sytem which underpinned most traditional African societies.

A few post colonial African leaders, such as Kwame Nkrumah, Julius Nyerere, Sekou Toure, Tserese Khama and Nelson Mandela, to their credit, drew considerably from these African traditions. Mandela writes in his memoir, *Long Walk to Freedom,*

"My notions of leadership were profoundly influenced by observing the regent and his court. I watched and learned from the tribal meetings that were regularly held at the great place." (21)

There is a strong case for arguing that abundance of raw materials, schooling and skills are not the primary cause of good government, economic development and healthy societies, as the case of Nigeria demonstrates, but rather its mental orientation and value system. Marcus Ramogale has noted that

"There is something within successful nations which prompts the people to do well – something higher than the 'profit motive'. You may call this a sound mental outlook and strong value system. To put it differently, a nation's 'psycho-cultural wealth' determines its success. If a nation's frame of mind is positive and orientated towards decency and excellence, then its education, training and work habits become effective, and indirectly, so does its economy and government."(22)

Just as the Japanese and Chinese leaders guided their people to a path of hard work, thrift and struggle against the tendency for shoddiness and mediocrity, African countries could be well-served by drawing upon the best elements of African traditional values systems to foster the sense of communal spirit in working towards structural economic change. However this drawing upon tradition values would need to absorb modern scientific knowledge in order to avoid culture becoming a dead weight.

Revolutions along the lines discussed are essential elements in achieving an African renaissance. For all African people, wherever they live, simply being African is challenging. The opportunity now is to transform the way African economies are run and how they relate to the rest of the world.

African people are faced with a historic challenge of industrialising their economies and developing a new self reliance. The dream of an African renaissance will remain only a dream until Africans, by their own efforts, face the challenge squarely, and in the process transform themselves.

References

(1) See Chinua Achebe's novel – Things Fall Apart
(2) For more discussion of Intellectual Warfare on Africans, see **Jacob H**
(3) **Carruthers;** 1999, **Martin Bernal;** 1987 and **Stephen Howe;** 1998
(4) See Albert Tevoedre; 2002
(5) **Achebe,** 2; 1988
(6) **Adam Hochschild,** 44; 1999
(7) **Cater Woodson,** *xiii,*1990
(8) **JH Clarke,** 46; 1994
(9) **Peter Wade,** 86; 1997
(10) **Amos Wilson,** 1-2; 1993
(11) **Martin Bernal,** 107; 1987
(12) **Chancellor Williams,** 19 and 21; 1987
(13) **Chancellor William,** opcit, 21,1987
(14) **JH Clarke,** 14; 1991 (see Notes for An African World revolution, 247; 1991
(15) **Chekh Anta Diop** , Black Africa, 116; 1987
(16) **Diop,** opcit 116,1987
(17) **JH Clarke,** 247; 1991
(18) **Peter Wade,** 86; 1997
(19) **Steve Biko,** 43;1988
(20)**Chinweizu,** 4; 1987
(21)**J.R.A Ayee,** public management in Africa ,(African Development Bank 's Economic working paper series 82, November 2005)
(22)**Nelson Mandela,** 19; 1994
(23)**Marcus Ramogale,** Africa – Quest for excellence,1998 www.Sairr.org.SA
Joel Kotkin, 1; 1992

SELECT BIBILIOGRAHY

Achuzia .JOG, *Requiem Biafra* ,(Nigeria, Enugu; 1986)

Achebe, C, *Hope and Impediment: Selected Essays* 1965-87,(Heinemann; 1988)

Action Aid, *Real Aid – An Agenda for Making Aid Work*(Action Aid; 2005)

Action Aid, *Money Talks: How Aid Conditions Continue to Drive Utility Privatisation in Poor Countries* (Action Aid; 2004)

Action Aid, Farmgate: *The Development Impact of Agrictultural Subsidies* (Action Aid; 2002)

Ake, Claude, *A political Economy of Africa* (Longman; 1981)

Ake, Claude, *The Marginalisation of Africa – Notes on a Productive Confusion* (Lagos;1996)

Ali-Akpajiak, Sofo and Pyke, Tony, *Measuring Poverty in Nigeria* (Oxfam Working papers; 2003)

Amamoo , JG, *The Ghana Revolution* (London; 1981)

Ani, Marimba , *YURUGU : An African – centered critique of Europe cultural Thought and Behaviour.* (Afrcan World press inc;1994)

Ayere, J.R.A, *Public Sector Management in Africa* (African Development Bank Economic Research Working Paper Series No, 82; 2005)

Bangura, Yusuf, *Structural Adjustment and the Political Question - Review of African Political Economy* (Review of African Political Economy; 1986)

Barratt-Brown, Micheal , *Africa's Choices* (Penguin; 1986)

Ben-Jochannan, *The Black Man of the Nile and His Family* (Black Classic Press)

Bernal, Martin, *Black Athena* (Vintage; 1987)

Biko, Steve, *I Write What I Like* (Penguin; 1988)

Birmingham, David (ed), *History of Central Africa: The Contemporary Years Since 1966* (Longman; 1998)

Carr, E.H , *What is History?* (Penguin; 1964)

Carruthers, Jacob, H , *Intellectual Warfare* (Third World Press; 1999)

Chaliand, Gerard , *The Struggle for Africa: Conflict of the Great Powers* (Macmillan; 1981)

Chamberlain, M.E, *The Scramble for Africa* (Longman; 1974)

Cheru, F, *Structural Adjustment, Primary Resource Trade and Sustainable Development in Sub-Saharan Africa* (World Development Vol.22, No. 10; 1989)

Chinweizu, *The West and The Rest of Us* (1974)

Chinweizu, *Decolonising the African Mind* (Pero Press; 1987)

Christian Aid Report, *Scorched Earth, Oil and War in Sudan* (www/christian-aid.org.uk; 2005)

Clarke, John. Henrik, *Who Betrayed the African World Revolution? And*

Other Speeches (Third World Press; 1997)

Clarke, John. **Henrik,** *Notes for an African World Revolution: Africans at the Crossroads* (Africa World Press; 1991)

Conway, Gordon, *The Doubly Green Revolution: Food For All in The 21st Century* (Penguin; 1994)

Curtis, Mark , *The Great Deception: Anglo-American Power and World Order* (Pluto Press 1998)

De Rivero, Oswaldo, *The Myth of Development* (Zed Press; 2001)

Devavajan, S, Dollar, D and Holmgren, T (ed), *Aid and Reform in Africa* (The World Bank; 2001)

De Witte, Ludo, *The Assassination of Lumumba* (Verso; 2001)

Diop, Cheikh. Anta, *The African Origin of Civilisation* ((Lawrence, Hill and Co 1974)

Diop, Cheikh. Anta , *Black Africa: The Economic and Cultural Basis for a Federated State* (Laurence Hill and Co; 1974)

Do Nascimento, Abdias, *Africans in Brazil* (African World Press; 1992)

Dumont, Rene, *False Start in Africa* (Earth Scan, London; 1988)

Fanon, Franz, *Towards an African Revolution* (Penguin; 1970)

Galbraith, JK, *The Nature of Mass Poverty* (Penguin;1980)

Gary, Ian, *Bottom of The Barrel: Africa's Oil Boom and the Poor* (Catholic Relief Services; 2003)

Green, R.H and Seedman, Ann, *Unity or Poverty? The Economics of Pan Africanism* (Penguin; 1968)

Guest, Robert, *The Shackled Continent* (Macmillan Ltd; 2004)

Gurley, John. G , *China's Economy and the Maoist Strategy* (Monthly Review Press; 1976)

Hayter, Teresa, *The Creation of World Povertyr* (Pluto Press; 1981)

Hilary, John, *Profiting from Poverty: Privatisation Consultants, DFiD and Public Services* (War on Want; 2004)

Hobsbawm, Eric, *The Age of Revolution* (Weidensfield and Nicolson; 1962)

Halliday, Jon , *Japanese Imperialism Today* (Monthly Review Press; 1973)

Howe, Stephen, *Afro-Centrism: Mythical Pasts and Imagined Homes* (Verso; 1998)

Iwe, N.S.S, Dr, Rev, *Christianity, Culture and Colonialism in Africa* (Undated

Jaffe, Hosea, *A History of Africa* (Zed Press; 1982)

Jaffe, Hosea,, *The Pyramid of Nations* (London; 1980)

James, C.L.R,, *Nkrumah and Ghana Revolution* (Allison and Busby Ltd; 1977

Kay, Cristobal , *Why East Asia Overtook Latin American Agrarian Reform, Industrialisation and Development* (TWQ, Vol 23, No.6, 1072-1102; 2002)

Keluejang, S.Anai, *The Myth of Freedom and Other Poems* (New Beacons,

1985)
Kotkin, Joel, *Tribes* (Random House, New York; 1992)
Kozul-Wright, Richard and Rayment, Paul, *Globalization re-loaded: an UNCTAD Perspective* (2004)
Lall, Sanjay, with Erika Kraemer-Mbula, *Industrial Competitiveness in Africa: Lessons from East Asia* (ITDG; 2005)
Liddle, R.William, *The Politics of Development Policy* (World Development, Vol. 20, No.6, 793-807; 1992)
Lockwood, Matthew, The State They're in: An Agenda for International Action on Poverty in Africa (ITDG; 2005)
MacKenzie, J.M, *The Partition of Africa* (Methuen, London; 1983)
Maier, Karl, *The House Has Fallen – Nigeria in Crisis* (Penguin; 2000)
Masden, Wayne, *Genocide and Covert Operations in Africa: 1993-1999* (NY Merlyn Press; 1992)
Mazrui, Ali, *The African: A Triple Heritage* (London; 1986)
M'buyiuga, Elenga, *Pan Africanism or Neo-Colonialism* (Zed Press; 1982)
Mkundawire, Thandika and Soludo, Charles, *Our Continent, Our Future: African Perspectives on Structural Adjustment)* (Africa World Press; 1999)
Nkrumah, Kwame, *Dark Days in Ghana* (PANAF; 1968)
Nkrumah, Kwame, *See Africa Must Unite* (PANAF; 1963)
Obasanjo, Olusegun, Obasanjo's Economic Directions;1999-2003 (Federal Secretariat at Abuja; 2000)
Ogbu, OM et al, *Technology Policy and Practice in Africa* (IDRC; 1995)
Okongwu, Chu. SP, *The Nigerian Economy: Being an Anatomy of a Traumatised Economy With Some Proposals For Stabilisation* (Enugu; 1984)
Onimode, Bade, *The Political Economy of African Crisis* (Zed Press; 1998)
Oyebola, A, *Black Man Dilemna* (Ibadan; 1976)
Pieterse, Jan Nederveen, *White on Black: Images of Africa and Blacks in Western Popular Culture* (Armistan; 1992)
Rodney, Walter, *How Europe Underdeveloped Africa* (Bogle-L'Ouvature, London; 1972)
Schumacher, E.F, *Small Is Beautiful* (Verso; 1990)
Sofola, J.A. *African Culture and The African Pesonality* (Ibadan; 1973)
Spencer, Claire, *The Maghreb in the 1990s: Political and Economic Developments in Algeria, Morocco and Tunisia* (Adelphi; 1992)
Stewart, Lall and Wagwe, *Alternative Development Strategies in Sub-Saharan Africa* (Macmillan; 1992)
Stiglitz, Joseph, E, *Globalisation and its Discontent* (Allen Lane; 2002)
Tevoedijre , Albert, *Winning the War Against Humilitation* (United Nations Development Programme; 2002)
Unctad, *Economic Development in Africa: Trade Performance and Commodity Dependence* (Unctad, New York; 2003)

Unwin, Tim, *Beyond Budgetary Support: Pro-Poor Development Agendas for Africa* (TWQ, Vol.25, No.8, 1501-1523; 2004)

Usman, Yusufu. **Bala,** *Nigeria Against the IMF* (Kaduna, Nigeria; 1986)

Van de Walle, Nicolas, *African Economies and The Politics of Permanent Crisis: 1979-1999* (Cambridge University Press; 2001)

Wade, Peter, *Race and Ethnicity in Latin America* (Pluto Press; 1997)

Wa Thiong, Ngugi, *The Crisis of Culture in Africa Today* (A speech to the African Society, Oxford University; 1982)

Watkins, Kevin, *Cultivating Poverty: The Impact of US Cotton Subsidies on Africa* (Oxfam; 2002)

Weber, Max, *The Protestant Ethic and The Spirit of Capitalism* (HarperCollins; 1991)

Willliams, Chancellor, *The Destruction of Black Civilisation* (Third World Press; 1987)

Wilson, Amos, *Afrikan-Centered Consciousness Versus The New World Order* (African World Infosystem, New York; 1998)

Wilson, Amos, *Blue Print for Black Power* (African World Infosystem, New York; 1999)

World Development Movement, *Zambia: Condemned to Debt – How the IMF and the World Bank Have Undermined Development* (www.wdn.org.uk/campaigns/debt/zambia/zambia.pdf; 2004)

Woodson, Carter, *The Miseducation of the Negro* (Africa World Press; 1990)

United Nations Development Program (UNDP) *Beyond Scarcity: Power, Poverty and the Global Water Crisis,* (Human Development Report; 2006)

Stein, Howard and Nafziger, Wayne *Structural Adjustment, Human Needs and the World Bank Agenda* (Journal of Modern African Studies, Vol 29.1; 1999)

Stubbs, Richards and Underhill,Geoffrey, *Political Economy and the Changing Global Order* (Macmillan; 1994)

Taylor, Ian, *China and Africa: Engagement and Compromise* (Routledge; 2006)

United Nations Development Program (UNDP) *Making New Technologies Work for Human Development,* (Human Development Report; 2001)

Unger, Craig, *House of Bush, House of Saud* (Gibson Square Books; London; 2005)

Yew, Lee Kuan, *From Third World to First – The Singapore Story: 1965-2000* (HarperCollins, New York; 2000)

Zakaria, Rafiq, *The Struggle Within Islam* (Penguin; 1988)

A

Abacha, General Sani 39, 71, 72, 78
Acheampong, Lt Col H.K. 26
Achuzia, Colonel Joseph 37
Adam Smith International 52
Ajaokuta 38
Alexander-The-Great 11
Ancient Egypt 11, 13, 14, 58, 93
Ani, Marimba 16
Appiah, Kwame 27, 28
Arabs 9, 15, 57, 58, 60, 61, 62, 63, 91
Awolowo, Chief Obafemi 25

B

Babangida, General Ibrahim 52, 72, 78
BAE Systems 87
Belewa., Abubaka Tafawa 71
Biafra 36, 37, 84, 104
Biafran Directorate of Research and Productivity 36
Black Africans 58, 59
Boukeflika, Abdelaziz 54
Britain 2, 26, 29, 45, 50, 52, 65, 75, 92, 95
Bushmen 15, 17

C

Cape Verde 11
Chevron Texaco 49
China 14, 18, 37, 39, 53, 54, 79, 95, 101, 105, 107
Chinese National Petroleum Company 49
Clarke, John Henry 73, 95
Clarke, Professor John Henrik 15
D
d'Estaing, Phillipe Giscard 37
Danjuma, Theophilus 26, 71, 72
Democratic Republic of Congo 14, 49, 65, 78
Djibouti 62
Dumont, Rene 34, 42

E

Emperor Haile Selassie of Ethiopia 14
European Union 46, 54, 58

108

Eyadema, Sergeant Gnassingbe 26

G

Geldof, Bob 87
General Mohammed Buhari 68
Ghana 12, 25, 26, 28, 31, 41, 46, 63, 76, 80, 104, 105, 106
Guinea Bissau 29

I

Ibos 36
International Monetary Fund 17, 43, 49, 68
Islamic Shiite Caliphate 63
Iwe, Dr Nwachukwuike 25

J

Japan 23, 24, 39, 65, 70, 75, 79, 86, 95

K
Kalu Idika Kalu 68
King Leopold of Belgium 90
Kwame Nkrumah 25, 26, 30, 31, 63, 75, 76, 102

L

Latin America 7, 15, 47, 107

M

MacKenzie, J.M 12
Millennium Summit 81
Morocco 48, 58, 61, 63, 106

N

Negritude 62
Neo-patrimonalism 30
Nigerian Civil War 36, 50, 84
Nigerian National Petroleum Corporation 65
North Africa 5, 57, 58, 59, 63, 64, 91
North Atlantic Treaty Organisation 17
Northern People's Congress 69

O

Obasanjo, General Olusegun 66, 68

Obukegi 14, 19, 38, 39, 89
Okigbo, Dr Pius 36
Onimode, Bade 35
Organisation of Islamic Conference 62
Oxfam 56, 87, 104, 107
Oyebola, Areoye 25, 26

P

Pharaoh Menkare 11
Price Waterhouse Cooper 51
profiteers. 31
Pygmies 15

R

Revolutionary Pan-Africanism 30
Rhodesia 15
Rivero, Oswaldo De 47
Royal Niger Company 23

S

Scramble for Africa 4, 5, 9, 43, 45, 47, 48, 49, 51, 52, 53, 54, 55, 104
Shell 49
Silicon Valley of the Middle East 85
Somalia 59, 61, 62, 85
South Africa 15, 29, 32, 33, 48, 55, 65
South Korea 23, 24, 70, 75, 78, 79, 80

T

Tanzania 31, 38, 45, 46, 52, 55, 80
Third World countries 45

U

United Nations Economic Commission for Africa 47

V
Voice of Zaire 37

W

Wilson, Amos 74, 88, 93, 103
World Bank 17, 43, 44, 47, 49, 51, 52, 53, 54, 55, 67, 69, 72, 77, 81, 105, 107
World Commission on Environment and Development 84

Z

Zaire 26, 37, 48, 78
Zambia 45, 48, 55, 107